GRAVES of Our FOUNDERS

Volume I

Their Lives, Contributions, and Burial Sites

JOE FARRELL • LAWRENCE KNORR • JOE FARLEY

Mechanicsburg, PA USA

Published by Sunbury Press, Inc.
Mechanicsburg, Pennsylvania

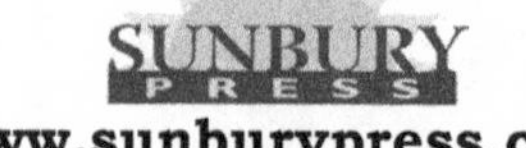

www.sunburypress.com

For information about special discounts for bulk purchases, please contact Sunbury Press Orders Dept. at (855) 338-8359 or orders@sunburypress.com.

To request one of our authors for speaking engagements or book signings, please contact Sunbury Press Publicity Dept. at publicity@sunburypress.com.

ISBN: 978-1-62006-176-3 (Trade paperback)

Library of Congress Control Number: 2018964337

FIRST SUNBURY PRESS EDITION: December 2018

Product of the United States of America
0 1 1 2 3 5 8 13 21 34 55

Set in Bookman Old Style
Designed by Crystal Devine
Cover by Lawrence Knorr
Edited by the authors

Continue the Enlightenment!

Contents

Introduction

Welcome to the first volume of a series of four books about the lives, contributions, and burial sites of this country's Founders. We have visited many graves and cemeteries over the past decade while writing eleven volumes of the Keystone Tombstones series and two volumes of Gotham Graves and our most recent book, *Murders, Massacres, and Mayhem in the Mid-Atlantic.* Typically we create a short biography of the person or persons, visit and photograph their grave and any other memorials that may be present or nearby, and chronicle it all in a chapter. On one of our field trips, we discussed writing a series of books covering the Founders of our nation. It seemed like a particularly good idea in light of the approaching 250th anniversary of the Declaration of Independence.

One of the first questions that arose is who is a Founder? We settled, at least for now, on signers of either the Continental Association, Declaration of Independence, Articles of Confederation or the Constitution, plus some other famous or noteworthy patriots who played a significant role in the creation of the United States of America. We have compiled a list of about 200 individuals who meet this criteria and are well on our way to visiting all of their graves.

These visits have been rewarding and exciting in many cases but also shocking and shameful in others. In the first instance, many Founders' life stories and contributions are little-known and we thoroughly enjoyed learning about them and in many cases experiencing a snippet of their lives. While the well-known like Washington, Hamilton, Sherman, and Adams have well-maintained, accessible graves, they are the exception rather than the rule. Many of our Founders are buried in places that are badly decayed and neglected, some are inaccessible and many cannot be located at all. They have been lost due to development of the land, decay, or poor record-keeping.

As a result of our experience visiting Founders' burial places, we decided to try to do something about this situation. We established a website, www.adoptapatriot.com, and continue to add information, data, and features that help call attention to this situation. We have contacted and continue to work with many organizations and public officials whom we think would be interested in this problem. The solutions are undetermined. We hope to call attention to Founders' graves that are weather-beaten and difficult to read, or in remote hard-to-find or reach locations, or under-memorialized given their role in our history. We have been calling for restoring, renewing, or relocating many of the graves but we will need help from local and regional persons or groups interested in doing so.

It is our hope that the stories contained in this and future volumes will shine a light on the contributions of the people who, in many cases, put their lives on the line in order to establish an independent nation. In particular we hope to light a fire of interest in our readers relative to those lesser-known Founders whose achievements have been largely forgotten.

It will be a difficult and costly task but we are inspired by a quote from Marcus Cicero that we ran across and used in our *Keystone Tombstones – Civil War* edition:

"Poor is the nation having no heroes;
shameful the one that having them, forgets."

George Washington
(1732–1799)

Cincinnatus Americanus

Buried at Washington family crypt,
"Mount Vernon" plantation, Mount Vernon, Virginia.

Continental Association • Commander in Chief • Military
U.S. Constitution • First President of United States

George Washington was a surveyor and soldier from a privileged Virginia family who rose to become the Commander in Chief of the Continental Army during the American Revolution and the first President of the United States. Dubbed "Father of Our Country," Washington was instrumental in leading the rebellious colonies to victory on the battlefield despite long odds and few supplies. He then held the young republic together through his nonpartisan approach during the formation of the new government following the adoption of the United States Constitution. The nation's capital and hundreds of other places and streets are named for him.

George Washington was born February 22, 1732 (new calendar), on the family estate "Wakefield" near Popes Creek in Westmoreland County, Virginia. He was the eldest of six children of Augustine Washington and his second wife Mary (née Ball) Washington. George, Samuel, Elizabeth (Betty), John Augustine, and Charles were siblings who survived to adulthood. Augustine was a wealthy planter, justice of the peace, and county sheriff who also had four children by his first wife Jane Butler. Only two of them survived to adulthood giving George two elder half-brothers: Lawrence and Augustine.

When George was three, the family moved to "Epsewasson," a plantation on the bluffs of the Potomac River. Three years later, the family moved to "Ferry Farm" near Fredericksburg where

Portrait of George Washington by Gilbert Stuart, circa 1797.

Washington spent most of his boyhood. It is this farm that was the location of the Parson Weems cherry tree legend. When George was 11, in 1743, his father passed away. He became the owner of "Ferry Farm" but was raised by his elder half-brother Lawrence at "Epsewasson" which was renamed to "Mount Vernon" in honor of British Vice Admiral Edward Vernon under whom Lawrence had served. Lawrence had married into the wealthy Fairfax family that same year, taking fifteen-year-old Anne Fairfax as his bride.

As a youth, Washington had private tutors and learned the art of surveying. Due to his brother's connections with Lord Fairfax, young George had many opportunities to utilize his surveying skills and became a land investor as a teenager. Also, due to his brother's service in the Virginia militia, George became interested in the military. In 1751, Lawrence became ill with tuberculosis. The two made a trip to Barbados with the hope the warm air would cure him. While there, George contracted smallpox but survived. This immunized him but left him with scars on his face. Unfortunately, Lawrence was not cured and passed away after returning to "Mount Vernon" in July of 1752. Nine years later, when his sister-in-law passed, George inherited "Mount Vernon."

Soon after his brother's death, George took his place in the Virginia militia, being named adjutant for the southern district of Virginia by Governor Robert Dinwiddie. Through 1758, he fought in the French and Indian War, including rallying the retreat of the ill-fated Braddock Expedition. In time, Washington rose to the head of the Virginia militia but in December 1758, he resigned his commission and returned to "Mount Vernon." He then married Martha Dandridge Custis, on January 6, 1759, a wealthy widow with two children, John Parke Custis and Martha Parke Custis, whom he raised as his own. George and Martha had no children of their own. The marriage also greatly increased his wealth and social standing.

George shelved the military life for a while and began a political career. He was a member of the Virginia House of Burgesses from 1758 to 1774 and a justice of the peace from 1760 to 1774. As the Revolution neared, he was elected to the First Continental Congress and was reelected to the Second. During this time, he signed the Continental Association and on June 14, 1775, following Lexington and Concord, was asked to serve as the commander of all continental forces. Washington appeared humbled by this appointment, thanking Congress for the opportunity but cautioned he was not experienced enough or prepared for the task. He graciously accepted, eschewing a salary and asking only his expenses to be paid. The Continental Congress chose capable subordinate officers to assist, including Major General Artemas Ward, Adjutant General Horatio Gates, Major General Charles Lee, Major General Philip Schuyler, Major General Nathanael Greene, Colonel Henry Knox, Colonel Alexander Hamilton, Colonel Benedict Arnold, and Brigadier General Daniel Morgan.

Washington took command of the army on July 2, 1775, at Cambridge, Massachusetts. He was astonished by how poorly prepared and undisciplined they were. He set about to correct these deficiencies. That September, he sent Arnold and 1000 troops to Canada to aid General Montgomery's siege of Quebec. The British reinforced the city, and the siege collapsed, forcing the Americans to retreat. Meanwhile, Washington proposed an attack on Boston, but his war council advised against it. He sent Henry Knox to retrieve cannons from the recently captured Fort Ticonderoga and had them placed on the Dorchester Heights in February 1776. General Howe then evacuated Boston.

Washington next moved his army to New York to fortify it, correctly predicting it would be the place of the next British attack. Howe resupplied in Nova Scotia and then headed to New York City. The two battled on Long Island in August, leading to another American retreat, this time under cover of darkness and fog to Manhattan. Washington considered abandoning Manhattan too, but generals Greene and Putnam urged him to defend it. Once again, Howe was victorious. Washington retreated to White Plains.

While Howe decided to stay in New York City for the winter, Washington crossed the Delaware into Pennsylvania as numerous enlistments were expiring and many were deserting. Howe split his army, placing a Hessian garrison in Trenton, New Jersey, to counter Washington's encampment. During Christmas of 1776, Washington launched a surprise attack on Trenton. He had boats gathered from up and down the river and then crossed the Delaware in heavy sleet and snow. At 8 AM on the 26th, the army attacked Trenton, surprising the Hessians there. Over 850 prisoners and supplies were taken and the Hessian colonel, Johann Rall, was killed. The Americans returned to Pennsylvania to consolidate their winnings and then headed back across the river on January 3rd, attacking British regulars at Princeton. Over 273 British were killed or captured to only 40 Americans killed or wounded. Washington himself led a counterattack coming within 30 yards of the British line. Howe's army retreated to New York City. Washington moved to Morristown, New Jersey, and camped for the winter.

The victories in New Jersey bolstered Washington's standing with Congress and led to many reenlistments. While in Morristown in early 1777, Washington had his army inoculated against smallpox. When British General Burgoyne moved south from Quebec to cut off New England, Howe decided to take Philadelphia instead of going up the Hudson to meet Burgoyne. At Brandywine, near Philadelphia, in September of 1777, the British outmaneuvered Washington and marched into Philadelphia. A subsequent attack on the British garrison at Germantown failed. Meanwhile, in upstate New York, General Gates defeated Burgoyne at Saratoga thanks to the aggressiveness of Generals Benedict Arnold and

Washington's home at Mount Vernon (photo by Lawrence Knorr).

Benjamin Lincoln. This led to the resignation of General Howe in May 1778 and brought the French into the war on the side of the colonies.

Now Washington found himself in a precarious position referred to as the Conway Cabal. Some in Congress wanted to replace Washington with Gates and several generals were involved in the intrigue. He ultimately survived this challenge and wintered with his army at Valley Forge in December 1777. Washington petitioned for more supplies for his men while the cold winter weather raged and many died from illness and starvation. Five congressmen came to visit the situation and by February 1778, supplies were in hand and the situation was improving.

In May 1778, with the alliance with France in place, the British retreated from Philadelphia and headed back to New York. Washington decided to attack them as they retreated, resulting in the Battle of Monmouth. British General Clinton, now the leader of the force, rebuffed the attacks and garrisoned at New York City. This was Washington's last battle in the north. He put little value in conquering cities and saw his objective as preserving his army.

Late in 1778, Clinton sent troops to Georgia to launch a southern invasion. He seized Savannah and then Charleston in January 1780, defeating General Lincoln. Clinton returned to New York and put General Cornwallis in charge. The British then moved deeper into South Carolina and routed Lincoln's replacement, Horatio Gates. Washington had recommended Nathanael Greene for the role, but Congress had disagreed. Now, they sent Greene, who proceeded to drag the British out in a costly campaign.

In the north, in the summer of 1779, Washington sent General Sullivan after the Iroquois, who were British allies. Sullivan routed the natives, the survivors fleeing to Canada. At Morristown, the winter of 1779-80 was harsh. While dealing with the deprivation of the cold winter, Washington was not aware that Benedict Arnold was betraying him. British spymaster John André had turned him earlier in the year. By the summer of 1780, Arnold hatched his plot to allow the British to take West Point, an important fort on the Hudson. That September, André was captured and the plot discovered. Washington offered the British André in exchange for Arnold, but they refused. Arnold became an officer in the British Army and André was executed at Tappan, New York, in October 1780. André had asked to be executed by firing squad, but Washington changed his mind to make an example of him. He was hanged instead.

As Greene was turning the tide in the south, Washington urged the French to join him in an attack on Cornwallis in Virginia in 1781. Washington feigned an attack on New York and headed south to the coast of Virginia. After the French naval victory in the Battle of the Chesapeake, the patriot forces trapped Cornwallis's army at Yorktown on October 19, 1781. Cornwallis failed to appear at the surrender, sending General Charles O'Hara instead. In response, Washington sent Benjamin Lincoln in his place.

The British then began a withdrawal from the colonies and the two sides started negotiating a peace treaty. By the fall of 1783, all the foreign armies were gone. Meanwhile, Washington's army was again in bad shape with the American treasury empty. Many soldiers were not paid and some of the officers considered a military coup. Known as the Newburgh Conspiracy, this unrest was put down in March 1783 as Washington got concessions from Congress. Washington later submitted his expenses for the war, totaling $450,000.

The Treaty of Paris was signed on September 3, 1783, officially recognizing the independence of the United States from Great Britain. On November 2, Washington disbanded his army and gave a farewell address to the troops. The British finally evacuated New York City on November 25, 1783. A little more than a week later, Washington bade farewell to his officers at Fraunces Tavern in New York City on December 4. Nearly three weeks later, on December 23, Washington resigned his commission before the Continental Congress which was convened in the Senate Chamber of the Maryland State House. Said Washington,

> I consider it an indispensable duty to close this last solemn act of my official life, by commending the interests of our dearest country to the protection of Almighty God, and those who have the superintendence of them, to his holy keeping.

Washington emulated the Roman consul Lucius Quintus Cincinnatus in relinquishing his military power to the state after victory. Historian Gordon Wood concluded it was "the greatest act of his life, the one that gave him his greatest fame." The Society of the Cincinnati was subsequently formed by Henry Knox with Washington as its first president. Upon resigning, Henry Knox took over as the new commander of the Continental Army. Washington then returned to "Mount Vernon."

Washington had been a proponent for a strong central government and was critical of the Articles of Confederation. When the Constitutional Convention was called in Philadelphia in 1787 to replace the Articles with a new Constitution, James Madison encouraged Washington to attend as a delegate from Virginia. His presence added legitimacy to the proceedings and he was named the president of the convention. Washington stayed out of any disputes and was non-partisan while others argued back and forth. When it came time to approve the Constitution for Virginia, Washington recused himself feeling it was inappropriate for him to vote for it when he was likely to be the first president.

In early 1789, the various states began ratifying the Constitution, but the March 4 deadline passed without a Congressional quorum to declare who had become President of the United States. Finally, there was a quorum on April 5 and the votes were counted on the 6th. Washington had been selected president and John Adams, with the second-highest vote tally, was to be vice president. Congressional secretary Charles Thomson rode to "Mount Vernon" to inform Washington.

Washington took the oath of office on April 30, 1789, at Federal Hall in New York City. Over 10,000 people attended the first inaugural parade as Washington arrived via coach escorted by a marching band and the militia. The oath was administered by Chancellor Robert R. Livingston. Washington then went about forming a government and setting many precedents including the preference of being referred to as "Mr. President" as opposed to "His Excellency" or "His Highness" as was common in royal courts. He selected Thomas Jefferson as Secretary of State, Alexander Hamilton as Secretary of the Treasury, Edmund Randolph as Attorney General, Samuel Osgood as Postmaster General, and Henry Knox as Secretary of War. In 1790, he moved the seat of government from New York to Philadelphia.

During his first term, political parties began to form and most of the government found itself in two camps led by Hamilton and Jefferson. Washington, though clearly in the Federalist camp allied with Hamilton, tried to stay above things and remain as nonpartisan as possible. Washington backed the concept of a central bank which was the subject of debate between the sides and led to a compromise that included moving the nation's capital to the shore of the Potomac River. He was planning to retire after one term but was concerned about the in-fighting and lack of stability in the government. Thus, he put himself up for re-election in 1792 and was elected unanimously in the electoral college. Adams was again vice president.

Washington assisted in the planning of the new capital and even helped lay the cornerstone in 1793 for the U.S. Capitol. In 1794, he rode at the head of an army as it crossed Pennsylvania for the Pittsburgh area in response to the Whiskey Rebellion. His personal commitment to put down the tax uprising further helped solidify the central government. After General St. Clair's failure three years prior, on August 24, 1794, General Anthony Wayne defeated the Northwest Indians at the Battle of Fallen Timbers, opening the Ohio country for settlement. On November 19, 1794, the Jay Treaty was signed with Great Britain, avoiding war and normalizing trade between the two countries. This greatly angered France and subjected Washington to more criticism than he had ever received from the Jeffersonians.

As Washington neared the end of his second term, he was relentlessly assailed by his political foes and a largely partisan press. He regarded the press as a disuniting force that spread falsehoods and even referred to them as "diabolical." Washington's term ended on March 3, 1797, when he was replaced by John Adams, who had narrowly defeated Thomas Jefferson. His farewell address to Congress reinforced the need for a strong central government and urged his successors to stay out of foreign entanglements. He returned to "Mount Vernon."

For more than a year, Washington enjoyed managing his plantation including a new distillery. However, he began to grow restless, especially when the French privateers began seizing American ships in 1798. He wrote to Secretary of War James McHenry offering his services to President John Adams. On July 4, 1798, Washington was offered the role of lieutenant general in charge of the armies. He accepted the position and held it until his death 17 months later. It was largely a ceremonial position as he delegated most responsibilities to Alexander Hamilton and did not assume field command. There was no invasion of the United States, as was feared.

The Washington tomb at Mount Vernon (photo by Lawrence Knorr).

On December 12, 1799, Washington rode out in the sleet and snow to inspect his plantation. He arrived late for dinner and did not change out of his wet clothes. By the next morning, he had developed a sore throat but still went out to mark some trees for cutting. That evening the sore throat had worsened, but he was still in good spirits. The following morning, his condition worsened and he had difficulty breathing. Doctors were summoned to treat him, drawing blood and foregoing a tracheotomy that might have saved him. He told his doctors as he sent them out of the room, "I die hard, but I am not afraid to go." His death came swiftly and

George Washington's sarcophagus (photo by Lawrence Knorr).

unexpectedly at approximately 10 PM on December 14. Martha was at his side. He was 67 years old.

George Washington was laid to rest in the family vault at "Mount Vernon" on December 18, 1799. It was mostly a private affair of close friends and family. Washington's good friend Henry "Light Horse Harry" Lee offered a eulogy on behalf of Congress. Said Lee, Washington was "first in war, first in peace, and first in the hearts of his countrymen." In his will, Washington freed all his slaves and directed that a new family vault be built at "Mount Vernon." This was finally completed in 1831. The following year it was debated in Congress that Washington should be buried in the capitol. However, on October 7, 1837, Washington's remains were placed, still in the original lead coffin, within a marble sarcophagus designed by William Strickland and constructed by John Struthers earlier that year. To this day, the outer vault has the sarcophagi of George and Martha Washington while the inner vault has the remains of other Washington family members and relatives.

Washington remains the most important figure in American history. He is now carved into Mount Rushmore and his name has been used for a state, the nation's capital, numerous counties, cities, townships, boroughs, streets, and ships. The Washington Monument, on the mall in Washington, D.C., was finally completed in 1885 in his honor.

During the bicentennial, on July 4, 1976, Washington was posthumously appointed to the grade of General of the Armies of the United States by Congressional resolution, effectively a six-star general. This restored his place as the highest-ranking military officer in U.S. history along with General John Pershing.

John Adams
(1735–1825)

Second to George

Buried beneath the First Unitarian Church,
Quincy, Massachusetts.

Continental Association • Declaration of Independence
Diplomat • Thought Leader • First Vice President
Second President

John Adams was not a real likable guy. His seemingly inborn contentiousness was a constraint in his political career. Yet he would serve in both Continental Congresses, sign the Declaration of Independence after a major role in its writing, serve as the United States' Ambassador to France, Holland, and Great Britain, and become America's first Vice President and second President. He made up for his irritating personality with honesty, competence, and hard work. What he lacked in popularity he made up in respect. Ben Franklin once wrote about Adams "I am persuaded that he means well for his country, is always an honest man, often a wise one, but sometimes, and in some things, absolutely out of his senses."

He was born in Quincy, Massachusetts in 1735, a fifth-generation New Englander. His father was a deacon and a town selectman. He was awarded a Harvard scholarship at age 16 and graduated in 1755 at the age of 20. His father expected him to become a clergyman but John chose law instead. In 1764 he married Abigail Smith. The marriage lasted 54 years and produced six children, one of which (John Quincy Adams) would become the sixth President in 1825. He made his first mark politically with his opposition to the Stamp Act in 1765. He wrote articles in the newspapers and gave speeches claiming the act invalid. He soon after moved to Boston and set up his law practice there.

Portrait of John Adams by Gilbert Stuart, circa 1815.

In 1770, Adams agreed to defend eight British soldiers charged with killing 5 civilians in what became known as the Boston Massacre. He justified taking on the very unpopular clients by claiming "It is more important that innocence be protected than it is that guilt be punished, for guilt and crimes are so frequent in this world that they cannot all be punished. But if innocence itself is brought to the bar and condemned, perhaps to die, then the citizen will say, 'whether I do good or I do evil is immaterial, for innocence itself is no protection,' and if such an idea as that were to take hold in the mind of the citizen that would be the end of security whatsoever." Adams won an acquittal for six of the soldiers and the other two, who had fired into the crowd, were convicted of manslaughter. Ultimately this enhanced his reputation as a courageous and fair man.

Adams was elected to the First Continental Congress in 1774 and then to the Second Continental Congress in 1775. In that year he nominated George Washington as commander-in-chief of the Continental Army. Publicly, Adams supported "reconciliation if practicable," but privately agreed with Ben Franklin that independence was inevitable. He opposed various attempts, including the Olive Branch Petition, aimed at trying to find peace between the colonies and Great Britain.

On June 7, 1776, Adams seconded Richard Henry Lee's resolution of Independence and backed it strongly until its passage on July 2. Congress appointed Adams, Thomas Jefferson, Benjamin Franklin, Robert Livingston, and Roger Sherman to draft the declaration. This Committee of Five decided at Adams' urging that Jefferson would write the first draft. Adams played an important role in its completion and it passed Congress on July 4.

Adams was soon serving on as many as ninety committees, chairing twenty-five, more than any other Congressman and in 1777 he became head of the Board of War and Ordnance, which oversaw the Continental Army. Late that same year he was named as commissioner to France and in February 1778 he sailed for Europe. He was to negotiate an alliance with the French who were debating whether or not to recognize and aid the United States. In 1779, Adams was one of the American diplomats to negotiate the Treaty of Paris, which brought an end to the Revolutionary War. After the war, he remained in Europe and from 1784 to 1785 he arranged treaties of commerce with several European nations. In 1785 he became the first U.S. minister to England.

In 1788, Adams returned home after nearly ten years in Europe. The following year, he was placed on the ballot for America's first presidential election. Partly because Adams had been out of the country on diplomatic missions, had not participated in the Constitutional Convention, and had not unduly antagonized anyone in America, he received thirty-four electoral votes coming in second to Washington. In accordance with the Constitution at the time, Adams was sworn in as Vice President. The same results occurred in 1792. Adams' two terms as vice president were politically uneventful and he grew increasingly frustrated with the position as he did not have much clout with Washington.

The election of 1796 was the first contested American presidential election. During Washington's two terms, deep philosophical differences had caused a rift and led to the formation of two parties: the Federalists and the Democratic-Republicans.

The Adams crypt beneath the United First Parish Church in Quincy, Massachusetts. John is on the left and Abigail on the right.

When Washington announced he would not be a candidate for a third term, an intense partisan struggle began. Adams was the Federalist nominee and Jefferson the opponent. Adams won with seventy-one electoral votes to sixty-eight for Jefferson who became vice president. Near the end of his term, he became the first President to occupy the newly constructed White House.

During Adams' term as President, the dominant issue was the threat of war with France who were angered over the Jay Treaty with England. France had supported the Americans during the revolution and now they were at war with England and resented our dealing with them. In response, the French navy began attacking American merchant ships. In 1797, President Adams sent diplomats to create a treaty with France. Upon arrival, three French diplomats, nicknamed "X," "Y," and "Z", proceeded to ask for bribes to start negotiations. The story made its way to the American public and over the next two years, the United States carried on an undeclared naval war with France. Although the country's ships fought many battles, war was never formally declared. To silence critics of the war with France, Congress passed the Alien and Sedition Acts in 1798. These acts were created as a way to punish those who criticize the American government with the intent to harm the government's position. These laws proved very unpopular.

In the election of 1800, Adams again faced Jefferson and Aaron Burr in what was a bitter campaign. The results were Jefferson and Burr receiving 73 electoral votes while Adams received 65. The election tie was decided by the House of Representatives and Jefferson declared the winner. Adams left town in the pre-dawn hours of March 4, 1801, and did not attend Jefferson's inauguration.

Adams and Jefferson reconciled in 1812 and corresponded with each other for years. Adams got to see his son become America's sixth President. Perhaps fittingly, the two Declaration of Independence signatories both died fifty years to the day of the adoption of the document on July 4, 1826. On his deathbed, the ninety-year-old Adams whispered, "Thomas Jefferson survives." It wasn't the case. Five hours earlier, the eighty-three-year-old Jefferson had died at Monticello.

Adams is buried in a family vault beneath the Unitarian Church in Quincy Massachusetts. Unlike Washington and Jefferson, there is no monument to him in the national capital.

Abigail Adams
(1744–1818)

Mrs. President

Buried beneath the First Unitarian Church,
Quincy, Massachusetts.

Thought Leader

Abigail Adams had a way with words. She was unique for her time. Without the benefit of any formal education, she was a forward thinker, an early advocate for women's rights, a vital confidant and advisor to her husband, the President of the United States, mother of John Quincy Adams, the sixth president, and the first First Lady to occupy the White House. She wrote many letters to her husband which were preserved and today serve to document much of the Revolutionary War home front and the Continental Congress. She is particularly famous for her March 1776 letter to John Adams and the Continental Congress, requesting they "remember the ladies, and be more generous and favorable to them than your ancestors. Do not put such unlimited power into the hands of the husbands. Remember all men would be tyrants if they could. If particular care and attention is not paid to the ladies we are determined to foment a rebellion, and will not hold ourselves bound by any laws in which we have no voice or representation." Extraordinary sentiment for the times. When John expressed some concern about George Washington's motives Abigail wrote: "If he was not really one of the best-intentioned men in the world, he might be a very dangerous one." John frequently sought the advice of Abigail on many matters and their letters are filled with intellectual discussions on government and politics.

Abigail Adams was born Abigail Smith in Weymouth, Massachusetts on November 11, 1744. Her father, William Smith,

Portrait of Abigail Adams by Jane Stuart after Gilbert Stuart, circa 1800.

was a Congregationalist minister and had a large private library. She was educated at home and the library was a big advantage. She was a straight-laced young lady who did not sing, dance, or play cards. For amusement, she read and wrote letters to friends and relatives. John and Abigail were third cousins and had known each other since childhood but around 1762 their relationship took a turn toward romance. Their courtship was slow. They were married by her father on October 25, 1764, when she was nineteen and he was just shy of twenty-nine. In the next twelve years, she gave birth to six children including future president John Quincy Adams.

After their reception they rode off on a single horse to their new home, the small cottage John had inherited. Later they moved to Boston, where his law practice expanded. In 1774, John moved the family to Braintree because the situation in Boston was increasingly unstable. In 1774 John went to Philadelphia to serve as his colony's delegate to the First Continental Congress. Abigail stayed home and the separation began a lifelong correspondence between them forming a rich archive of their relationship and a chronology of the public issues debated and confronted by the new nation's leaders. It is believed that over the years they exchanged over 1100 letters.

As the Declaration of Independence was being debated at the Second Continental Congress Abigail began to press the argument in her letters that the creation of a new form of government was an opportunity to make the legal status of women equal to men. These are some of the earliest known writings calling for women's equal rights. John listened but she was never able to convince him.

As the separation lasted through the revolution Abigail was responsible for raising the children and running the farm and took responsibility for the family's financial matters. All of which she did very well. In 1778 John was named as minister to France and then in 1785 was named the first U.S. minister to England. Until she joined him in 1783, she kept him informed of domestic politics while he confided international affairs to her. When she joined him in Europe she was at first intimidated by the novel experience of Paris but grew to like it. She disliked London where she felt she received a cold shoulder by polite society. One pleasant experience during this time was her temporary guardianship of Thomas Jefferson's daughter Mary (Polly). They formed a deep and lifelong friendship. In 1788 she and John returned to a house in Quincy, Massachusetts which she enlarged and remodeled. It is still standing and open to the public as part of Adams National Historic Park.

When John became Vice President in 1789 Abigail stayed with him in the capital for only part of the time, often returning to Massachusetts to look after their farm and to tend to other business matters. When she was in the capital (New York), she helped First Lady Martha Washington with entertaining dignitaries. John Adams was inaugurated as the second President of the United States on March 4, 1797, in Philadelphia. Abigail did not attend as she was tending to John's dying mother. She remained a supportive spouse and confidante during his presidency although she incurred a lot of criticism for her involvement with politics. She was accused of advocating war with France, writing pro-administration editorials and asking others to get similar articles published, supporting laws that were unpopular, and promoting public education for women. She did not hesitate to speak her mind which was difficult for some critics to accept. Her political opponents came to refer to her as "Mrs. President."

She was the first First Lady to live in the White House although for only four months, arriving in November 1800. During that time she famously hung her family's laundry in the unfinished East Room to dry. After John's defeat in his presidential reelection campaign, the family returned to Quincy in 1800. Abigail continued to run the farm and care for family members, including their eldest child Nabby who died of cancer at their home in 1814.

For seventeen years, she and John shared time together. She continued a lively correspondence with many people and even resumed writing Thomas Jefferson after hearing of his daughter's death. This also opened a new friendship between John and Thomas Jefferson. She would not live to see her son John Quincy elected President in 1824. She died of typhoid fever on October 28, 1818. She is buried beside her husband in a crypt located in the First Unitarian Church in Quincy. In 1840 her grandson Charles published 114 of her letters and in 1876 he edited the wartime correspondence between John and Abigail.

William Blount
(1749–1800)
Founder of Tennessee

Buried at First Presbyterian Church Cemetery,
Knoxville, Tennessee.

U.S. Constitution • First Governor Southwest Territory

William Blount was a signer of the Constitution, the only governor of the Southwest Territory which shortly became the state of Tennessee, and one of the first two Senators from Tennessee. He played a leading role in forming that state but was embroiled in an international conspiracy that ruined his reputation on the national level. However, Blount always remained popular in his home state.

Born on Easter Sunday, March 26, 1749, to Jacob Blount and Barbara Gray Blount, he was the eldest child of well-to-do plantation owners at "Rosefield" near Windsor, Bertie County, North Carolina. Soon after, Jacob Blount built the plantation "Blount Hall," in Pitt County, North Carolina. William was a descendant of Captain James Blount of Albermarle County, North Carolina, who was one of the leaders of Culpeper's Rebellion in 1677. He was also a descendant of King John of England and related to Lady Elizabeth Blount who bore an illegitimate son with King Henry VIII.

Blount's mother, Barbara Gray, was the daughter of the owner of "Rosefield," Scottish businessman John Gray. Jacob and Barbara had six more children after William: Anne, John Gray, Louisa, Reading, Thomas, and Jacob. Following Barbara Gray's premature death, Jacob married Hannah Salter, and they had five children, though only Willie and Sharpe lived to adulthood.

The Blount children were not formally educated, but the sons gained experience managing their father's plantation. Jacob

Portrait of William Blount (circa 1828–1884) by Washington Bogart Cooper.

taught his sons the profit potential of land speculation while raising livestock, cotton, and tobacco.

In the late 1760s and early 1770s, the Blount family was loyal to North Carolina Governor William Tryon. Jacob, a justice of the peace, provided supplies for Tryon's army prior to the Battle of Alamance in 1771. William, Jacob, and John Gray marched in Tryon's army. Many early historians called this battle the first of the American Revolution, though this point of view has faded in more recent times because the uprising was not an attempt to gain independence from the king, but rather to protest local corruption.

As tensions increased with England, the Blounts became patriots. Early in the Revolution, father Jacob and William were regimental paymasters for different militia districts in North Carolina. While not an officer, William was paid as if he were a captain. The family also contributed provisions to the cause. William was with

George Washington in 1777 at the defense of Philadelphia and later helped defend Charleston against the British siege in 1780.

In 1778, William married Mary Grainier (Granger). The couple had six children; Ann, Mary Louisa, William Grainger, Richard Blackledge, Barbara, and Eliza.

William began running for a state House of Commons seat in 1779 but lost to Richard Dobbs Spaight in a contested election after a bitter battle. Eventually, the election results were voided due to proof of fraud. Meanwhile, in 1780, Blount was the official commissary to General Horatio Gates who oversaw the southern colonial forces. Blount was present when Gates lost the Battle of Camden in August of that year. Over $300,000 of soldier's pay was lost in the confusion of battle.

Blount ran again for the House of Commons seat in 1781 and won. In 1782, he was elected as one of North Carolina's four delegates to the Continental Congress. There he helped defeat new taxes and was for a strong army. He also introduced a bill known as the "Land Grab Act," which opened North Carolina's lands west of the Appalachians to settlement. Many soldiers used their grants to acquire land in this Tennessee Valley, or they sold them to the Blounts or other speculators. In 1784, Blount sponsored a bill that established the city of Nashville. He also sponsored a bill offering these lands to the Continental Congress to pay off North Carolina's war debts. While this narrowly passed, opponents repealed the act later in the year. However, in the meantime, a movement to establish the State of Franklin was underway led by John Sevier.

In 1785 and 1786, he worked to prevent the Hopewell Treaty that granted the Indians sizeable lands North Carolina speculators were hoping to retain. In 1787, Blount was a candidate for president of the Congress but lost to Arthur St. Clair. In March of that year, Blount was one of five delegates from North Carolina to the Constitutional Convention in Philadelphia. He joined the convention in June, after it had started, and went back and forth between the Continental Congress and the convention, returning for final debates. Gouverneur Morris convinced Blount to sign the Constitution. Confident it was better for North Carolina, he then campaigned for its ratification in his home state which occurred in 1789.

Though Blount lost his race for Senate from North Carolina in November 1789, he continued to work on the creation of the Southwest Territory which included the so-called State of Franklin. In 1790, the Southwest Territory was formally created

The mansion of William Blount in downtown Knoxville, Tennessee (photo by Lawrence Knorr).

and President George Washington appointed William Blount as governor. William was sworn in at "Mount Vernon." Blount then went about organizing the territory. In 1791, he began construction of his mansion in the new city of Knoxville. He also negotiated the Treaty of Holston that year which brought thousands of acres of Indian lands under U.S. control. Despite the treaty, tensions continued with the Indians and western settlers.

Blount then began implementing the steps required for statehood. This was achieved in early 1796. Blount realized he would lose an election to be the first governor to Sevier so he sought one of the two Senate seats from the new state. He was successful and represented the new state of Tennessee in Washington, D.C., when it was accepted into the union on May 31, 1796.

Meanwhile, during the early years of the republic, the Blount brothers had been accumulating lands in the west, amounting to over 2.5 million acres by the time he took his seat in the Senate. When land prices collapsed in 1795 following France's defeat of Spain in the War of the Pyrenees, the family went deeply into debt. William and his family attempted to sell lands to English investors but failed. Many feared the French would gain control of Louisiana and shut off American access to the Mississippi River.

To counter this, and to try to preserve his land values, Blount worked behind the scenes to convince the British to attack and take control of Florida and Louisiana. Blount's secret activities were betrayed when a letter spelling out the conspiracy made its way up the chain to President John Adams in early 1797. Adams sent the letter to the Senate where it was presented on July 3, 1797, while William was out. When he returned, the clerk read the letter aloud to Blount's stunned silence. Vice President Thomas Jefferson, who was sitting in the Senate, questioned Blount about the veracity of the letter, but Blount stammered for a postponement. This was granted.

William did not return the next day, but sent his fellow senator from Tennessee, William Cocke, to request more time again. This was rejected, and the Senate began an investigation. Blount tried to flee but was seized and testified before the committee, denying he wrote the letter. On July 8, the House of Representatives voted to hold impeachment hearings and the Senate voted 25 to 1 to sequester Blount's seat, effectively booting him from the body.

Blount left for home. The rest of the conspiracy came to light over the ensuing months. In early 1798, during Blount's impeachment hearing, a brawl erupted between congressman Matthew Lyon (Vermont) and Roger Griswold (Connecticut). On January 11, 1799, the Senate voted to dismiss the impeachment, arguing that such actions from the House do not affect Senators.

The "Blount Conspiracy" destroyed William's reputation and touched off a series of accusations between Federalists and Anti-federalists. George Washington hoped Blount would be "held in detestation by all good men." Abigail Adams called the conspiracy a "diabolical plot," and bemoaned the fact that there was no guillotine in Philadelphia. Others suggested the conspiracy was part of a greater French plot orchestrated by Thomas Jefferson or that it was an attempt to blackmail Spain.

While William was finished at the national level, he remained popular in his new home state of Tennessee where he was given a hero's welcome in September 1797. He became involved with the state Senate and was named Speaker in late 1798.

In March 1800, an epidemic hit the area. While William tended to his family, he also fell ill on March 11. He died on the night of March 21, 1800, and is buried at the First Presbyterian Church Cemetery a short distance from his Knoxville home.

Blount County, Tennessee is named after William and several towns, forts, schools, and streets are named after him, his wife, or

The worn slab covering the grave of William Blount. (photo by Lawrence Knorr).

other family members. Blount Mansion still stands in downtown Knoxville and provides a museum dedicated to the Blount family. Blount is also honored by a bronze statue in the "Signers' Hall" exhibit at the National Constitution Center in Philadelphia and by a plaque on the first-floor rotunda of the North Carolina State Capitol.

Brother Thomas Blount represented North Carolina in the U.S. House of Representatives in the 1790s and 1800s. Half-brother Willie Blount was Governor of Tennessee from 1809 to 1815. The Blount children remained in politics or married prominently. William Grainger Blount represented Tennessee in the U.S. House of Representatives from 1815 to 1819. Mary Louisa Blount married Congressman Pleasant Miller, and Barbara Blount married General Edmund P. Gaines.

Aaron Burr
(1756–1836)
Rival of Hamilton

Buried at Princeton Cemetery,
Princeton, New Jersey.

Military • Third Vice President

He is said to be one of the most brilliant students to graduate from Princeton in the 18th century. He served his country with distinction during the American Revolution. He was instrumental and perhaps the man most responsible for Thomas Jefferson's election to the office of President of the United States. He served as Vice President during Jefferson's first term but is most remembered for killing the former Secretary of the Treasury Alexander Hamilton in America's most famous duel. He is the only Founder who was ever tried for treason and one of his biographers, Nancy Isenberg, titled her work *Fallen Founder.* Of all the Founders he could easily be singled out as the most historically maligned and misunderstood. He was born on February 6, 1756, in Newark, New Jersey and named Aaron Burr.

Burr's father the Reverend Aaron Burr was pastor of the First Presbyterian Church of Newark. He was also the second President of the College of New Jersey now known as Princeton. His mother, Esther Edwards Burr, was the daughter of Jonathan Edwards a famous minister noted for his beliefs in the teachings of John Calvin. Burr's father taught mathematics and ancient languages in addition to raising funds for the college. Before Burr reached his second birthday his very successful father caught a fever and passed away in 1757. Shortly after, Burr's mother died after coming down with smallpox. Burr and his orphaned sister Sally were sent to Elizabethtown to live with their uncle Timothy Edwards who was a strict Puritan.

Portrait of Aaron Burr, 1802, by John Vanderlyn.

Burr didn't get along well with his uncle and tried to run away several times. At just eleven years of age, Burr presented himself as a prospective student to the college where his father had served as president. By all accounts, he was not even permitted to take the entrance exam that his father had created years before. He was rejected on the basis of being too young and too small. Two years later he was accepted at Princeton and graduated in 1772 at the age of eighteen. After briefly studying for the ministry, Burr decided that life was not for him and he traveled to Connecticut where he studied law at a school that had been established by his brother-in-law Tapping Reeve.

When the Revolution began, Burr was quick to join the American cause. Congress approved an assault on Canada where troops led by Colonel Benedict Arnold would join forces led by Brigadier General Richard Montgomery in an attack on Quebec. Burr joined and served under Arnold's command on an arduous

600-mile march over unforgiving terrain to Quebec. He performed so well on this difficult journey that when Arnold and Montgomery joined forces, Burr was made a captain on the headquarters staff.

The actual assault of Quebec was led by Montgomery and Burr marched beside him. Grapeshot mortally wounded Montgomery who died in Burr's arms. Burr's attempts to rally the men behind him to continue the attack were countermanded by Montgomery's second in command. Montgomery's forces retreated and Arnold's were also overwhelmed. The assault on Quebec ended in failure but Burr's courage in the face of fire earned him the admiration of all those around him. A story, there is no way of knowing whether it is true, spread that as the retreat began the five-foot-six-inch Burr hoisted the body of his much larger commander on his shoulders and tried to retreat through deep snow before having to abandon his burden to avoid capture.

Upon his return home, with his fame having preceded him, Burr was offered and accepted a position on George Washington's staff. At the time Washington was preparing the defense of the city of New York. The two did not mesh. Though Burr was young, he was well-educated and had studied military tactics. He viewed Washington as an inexperienced Indian fighter who had yet to win a battle. Burr was quickly transferred as an aide to General Israel Putman where he received high marks for his valor and sound judgment.

Burr and Washington also clashed at the Battle of Monmouth fought in June 1778 in New Jersey. At one point Washington refused to allow Burr to lead an attack on a British position that Burr felt could have been easily taken. The battle itself was fought in intense summer heat and Burr suffered sunstroke. Burr requested and was granted a short leave of absence but his health failed to improve as quickly as he had hoped. On March 10, 1779, Washington accepted Colonel Burr's resignation with regrets. He retired with solid credentials as a hero of the Revolution.

In April of 1782, Burr set up a law practice in Albany. That same year he married the widow of a formal colonel in the British army, Theodosia Prevost. At age 36, Burr's new wife was ten years his senior and already the mother of five. Despite their age difference, the couple was happily married. One year later, she bore Burr a daughter who was named after her mother. Burr was totally devoted and attentive to both Theodosias. As a husband

and father, even his worst enemies could find little in the way of criticism relative to his behavior.

Once peace with England was achieved, Burr moved his family back to New York and it was here his political career began. Within six months of his arrival, he was elected to the State Assembly. After serving his term during which he supported the abolition of slavery in New York, he returned to the practice of law. His knowledge and ability soon made him one of the leaders of the state bar. Another hero of the Revolution by the name of Alexander Hamilton was also a rising star in New York's legal circles. Though they disagreed fundamentally when it came to politics, both Burr and Hamilton respected each other during these years.

In 1789, Burr was appointed to the office of Attorney General for the State of New York by Governor Clinton. In 1791, with the support of two politically powerful New York families, the Clintons and the Livingstons, Burr was elected to the United States Senate defeating Hamilton's father-in-law Philip Schuyler. One of the reasons the Clintons and Livingstons backed Burr over Schuyler was the fact that in their view Hamilton had used his influence in the Washington administration to deny public offices to both families. Still, Hamilton did not direct his venom at those most responsible for the Schuyler defeat. Instead, he zeroed in on Burr. In the words of one of Burr's biographers, Milton Lomask, from this point on Hamilton's letters "would be filled with excoriations of Burr, with those flashes of naked hatred . . ."

In 1794, Burr's wife died after suffering a prolonged illness. Burr had come close to resigning his Senate seat in order to be with her in her last days. One of the things that may have stopped him was a letter he received from his eleven-year-old daughter who informed Burr that his wife was begging him not to leave Congress.

In the Presidential election of 1796, Burr received thirty electoral votes. When his Senate term ended, he returned to New York to restart his legal practice. He also busied himself strengthening New York's Republican party in preparation for the election of 1800. During the election, Burr once again outmaneuvered Hamilton and New York's electoral votes were instrumental in giving Thomas Jefferson the votes needed to capture the presidency. As it turned out, the Republicans nationwide were loyal to their candidates as Jefferson and Burr both received 73 electoral votes which threw the election to the House of Representatives. After thirty-six ballots, the House elected Jefferson and Burr was elected Vice President. Almost immediately, Burr was charged by various newspapers and pamphleteers with having plotted with Federalists to try to steal the presidency from Jefferson. This was highly unlikely as in fact had Burr desired to make a deal with the opposition party he probably could have done so easily as many Federalists preferred him to Jefferson. Still, the charges, which may have been inspired by Hamilton, drove a wedge between Jefferson and his Vice President.

The grave of Aaron Burr at Princeton Cemetery, Princeton, New Jersey (photo by Lawrence Knorr).

By 1804 Jefferson had decided to remove Burr as his running mate. As a result, Burr ran for the office of Governor of New York. He was defeated in a bitterly contested race and ultimately came to blame scandalous attacks on his character by Federalists in general and Hamilton specifically for the loss. Burr wrote Hamilton a letter demanding a retraction of the charges that had been made against his character. The two exchanged correspondence but the matter was not settled peacefully. On July 11, 1804, Burr killed Hamilton in a duel. That meeting, perhaps the most famous duel in history, effectively ended Burr's political life as well as Hamilton's earthly existence.

After the duel, Burr returned to Washington to finish his term as Vice President. By all accounts, he handled these duties admirably. One of his final acts was presiding over the Senate impeachment trial of Supreme Court Justice Samuel Chase. It was no secret that Jefferson wanted Chase, a Federalist, removed from office. Burr was praised for the fair manner in which he conducted the trial. As a matter of fact, his conduct presiding over the trial drew praise from even those who had been critical of him. He was described as performing his duties "with the dignity

Detail of Burr's tombstone (photo by Lawrence Knorr).

and impartiality of an angel, but with the rigor of a devil." Chase was acquitted on all counts. Historians point to this case as the one that established the independence of the American judiciary.

In 1807, Jefferson had Burr arrested and tried on charges of conspiracy to lead an attack on territory under Spanish control and trying to separate those territories from the United States. He was acquitted of all charges. After the trial, Burr traveled to Europe where he lived for years before returning to America where he died at the age of eighty in 1836.

Perhaps it is time for Americans to judge Burr on his service to his country during the Revolution and in public office rather than on his duel with Hamilton. In fact we may want to remember him for his farewell remarks to the Senate as Vice President when he said that the Senate was a "sanctuary; a citadel of law, of order, and of liberty . . . and if the Constitution be destined ever to perish by the sacrilegious hands of the demagogue or the usurper, which God avert, its expiring agonies will be witnessed on this floor." After Burr left the room one of the senators who heard the speech reported that there was solemn and silent weeping for a full five minutes after Burr's exit.

Daniel Carroll

(1730–1796)

A Catholic Patriot

Buried at St. John the Evangelist Church Cemetery,
Forest Glen, Maryland.

Articles of Confederation • U.S. Constitution

Daniel Carroll was a politician from Maryland and one of our Founding Fathers. He was a prominent member of one of the United States' great colonial Catholic families, whose members included his younger brother, Archbishop John Carroll, the first Roman Catholic bishop in the United States and founder of Georgetown University; and their cousin Charles Carroll of Carrollton, who signed the Declaration of Independence. Daniel was reluctant at first to get involved in the patriot cause because he was concerned that the Revolution might fail and as a rich slaveholder and large landowner he would be ruined. He gradually got over this fear and joined the cause to become one of five men to sign both the Articles of Confederation and the Constitution.

Daniel Carroll was born on July 22, 1730, in Upper Marlboro, Maryland to a wealthy family. He spent his early years at "Darnall's Chance," a plantation of 27,000 acres which his mother Eleanor Darnall Carroll had inherited from her grandfather. Several acres of this estate are now a museum and it is listed in the National Register of Historic Places. Between 1742 and 1748 he studied at the College of St. Omer in French Flanders, a Jesuit school established for the education of English Catholics. He then went on a tour of Europe and returned home where he soon married Eleanor Carroll, a first cousin of Charles Carroll of Carrollton.

For about the next 20 years Carroll was slowly and gradually converting to the patriot cause. He believed that if the colonists

Portrait of Daniel Carroll etched by Albert Rosenthal, 1888, based on a photograph of a painting.

failed in their effort to win their independence he would face financial ruin.

Catholics were prohibited from holding office at that time by colonial laws. After the laws were nullified in 1776 by the Maryland Constitution, Carroll was elected to the Maryland Senate and served from 1777 to 1781. As a state senator, he helped raise troops and money for the American cause.

He was then elected to the Continental Congress and served there from 1781 until 1784. In 1781 towards the end of the Revolution, he signed the Articles of Confederation, which formally established the United States.

In 1787 Carroll was named a Maryland delegate to the Philadelphia Convention which convened to revise the Articles of Confederation and produced the Constitution. He had become good friends with both George Washington and James Madison and like them believed that a strong central government was needed to regulate commerce among the states and with other nations. He wanted the power of the government to be vested in the people. He served on the Committee on Postponed Matters and spoke about 20 times in the debates at the Convention. He spoke out repeatedly in opposition to the payment of members of Congress by the states and when it was suggested that the president should be elected by Congress, Carroll moved that the words "by the legislature" be replaced with "by the people". He was the author of the presumption–enshrined in the Constitution—that powers not specifically delegated to the federal government were reserved to the states or to the people. Carroll and Thomas Fitzsimons were the only Catholics to sign the Constitution but

The grave of Daniel Carroll at St. John the Evangelist Catholic Church Cemetery in Forest Glen, Maryland (photo by Lawrence Knorr).

their signing was a symbol of the advance of religious freedom in America.

After the convention, he returned to Maryland and campaigned for ratification but was not a delegate to the Maryland state convention. He defended the Constitution in the *Maryland Journal*, often in opposition to the arguments of the well-known Maryland anti-Federalist Samuel Chase. He ended one of his letters to the paper by saying "Regarding it then in every point of view with a candid and disinterested mind I am bold to assert that it is the best form of government which has ever been offered to the world." After the Constitution was ratified, Carroll was elected to the First Congress of 1789, meeting in New York City and representing the Sixth Congressional District of Maryland. There he voted for the assumption of state debts accumulated during the war by the federal government. This was part of a "grand bargain" proposed by the U.S. Secretary of the Treasury Alexander Hamilton and agreed to by Secretary of State Thomas Jefferson. Part of the bargain was the locating of the new national capital in the upper South along the Potomac River.

In 1791, George Washington named his friend Daniel Carroll as one of three commissioners to survey and define the District of Columbia, where Carroll owned much land. The new United States Capitol was to be built on the wooded hill owned by his nephew. As one of his first official acts as commissioner, on April 15, 1791, he and David Stuart of Virginia, a fellow commissioner laid the cornerstone for the beginning boundary line of the District at Jones Point, on the south bank of the Potomac. He served as a commissioner until 1795, when he retired because of poor health.

In the last year of Carroll's life, he became a partner with George Washington in their Patowmack Company. The intent of this company was to link the middle states with the west by means of a Potomac River canal. Daniel Carroll died on May 7, 1796, at the age of 65 at his home in the present village of Forest Glen. He was interred at St. John the Evangelist Catholic Cemetery there.

Samuel Chase
(1741–1811)
First to be Impeached

Buried at Old St. Paul's Cemetery,
Baltimore, Maryland.

Continental Association • Declaration of Independence
Supreme Court Justice

In 1766 town officials in Annapolis, Maryland published an article in the *Maryland Gazette Extraordinary* that described one young citizen as "a busy, restless incendiary, a ringleader of mobs, a foul-mouthed and inflaming son of discord and faction, a common disturber of the public tranquility, and a promoter of the lawless excesses of the multitude." The man who may well have embraced the description would later serve in the Continental Congress, sign the Declaration of Independence, and serve as an Associate Justice on the United States Supreme Court. Born on April 17, 1741, his name was Samuel Chase.

Chase's background and upbringing were not what one would expect of a fiery revolutionary. His father was an Episcopalian clergyman who moved to what was then the village of Baltimore to minister to the congregation of St. Paul's Church. His mother, Matilda, passed away soon after giving birth to the couple's only son. Chase was homeschooled by his father before leaving for Annapolis to study law. He was admitted to the bar in 1761. He started a law practice and soon earned the reputation of a man unafraid to speak his mind regardless of whom, including the rich and powerful, might be offended. He had a reddish-brown complexion that seemed to grow more colorful when he engaged in a debate or argument. This trait earned him the nickname "Bacon Face."

Portrait of Samuel Chase, circa 1811, by John Wesley Jarvis.

In 1762 Chase married Ann Baldwin and the couple had seven children though only four survived to adulthood. Ann passed away in 1776 and Chase remarried eight years later. The second Mrs. Chase was the daughter of an English physician and she bore the American patriot two daughters.

Chase got his start in politics when he was elected to the Maryland General Assembly in 1764. He was also active in a group known as the Sons of Liberty whose purpose was to protect American colonists from oppressive British laws. This was close to the heart of the young Chase. After the Stamp Act was passed in 1765, Chase led a group of fellow patriots on a raid of public offices in Annapolis where they destroyed the stamps and burned the tax collector in effigy. Criticized publicly by the Loyalist mayor for these acts, Chase responded in the newspaper where he admitted to taking part in the raid adding that he did so while others who shared his beliefs "meanly grumbled in your corners and not daring to speak your sentiments." He was 24 years old at the time.

Though he may not have been popular with local officials his reputation among patriots earned him an appointment to the First Continental Congress in 1774. When it came to the work of Congress, Chase was a popular member owing to his willingness to serve on multiple committees and his effectiveness in carrying out his duties. He remained a member of Congress until 1778.

In 1776 Chase returned from Canada with Charles Carroll and Benjamin Franklin after the trio had been unsuccessful in convincing those colonies to provide military support in the Revolutionary War. Back in Maryland, the legislature had yet to decide on how the state should vote on the question of American independence. Chase returned to his home state to lobby support for separation from England. Thanks in part to his efforts, Maryland instructed its delegation to vote in favor of independence.

Chase, much to his chagrin, was not present when the historic vote was taken. He remained in Maryland tending to his ailing wife until the middle of July. It wasn't until August 2, in what may well have been his proudest moment, that he was able to affix his signature to the Declaration of Independence.

In 1778 Chase left Congress after being discredited in newspapers for using inside information to profit from the wartime flour market. Returning to Maryland he made a number of bad investments that left him bankrupt. He went back to practicing law in order to remedy his financial situation.

In 1787 Chase declined an appointment to the Constitutional Convention. By this time he was leading a campaign in Maryland for paper money emission, a matter of vital importance when it came to his personal finances as a result of debts he had incurred while speculating on confiscated estates of those who had remained loyal to the English. When the ratification of the Constitution was debated in Maryland, Chase, joined by fellow Declaration of Independence signer William Paca, opposed it. George Washington and James Madison used their influence in the state to overcome the objections raised by Chase and Paca.

After the Constitution was ratified Chase became a firm Federalist and supporter of the new government. On January 26, 1796, President Washington appointed Chase to the United States Supreme Court. Though he was now a member of the

The worn tombstone of Samuel Chase at Old St. Paul's Cemetery in Baltimore, Maryland (photo by Lawrence Knorr).

nation's highest court this exalted position did nothing to curb his tendency, some might say need, to express his views. Some held that he bullied defendants and their lawyers. Nor was he shy about continuing to express his political views.

When Thomas Jefferson was elected President in 1800, Chase was an unapologetic critic of the nation's new leader. He said that under Jefferson's leadership "our Republican Constitution will sink to mobocracy, the worst of all possible governments." Jefferson was determined to purge the judiciary of Federalist judges. Urged by the President, the House of Representatives impeached Chase for allegedly showing extreme partisan conduct while on the bench while deciding several cases. Chase was the first and only Supreme Court Justice ever impeached. His trial took place early in 1805 with the United States Senate presided over by then Vice President Aaron Burr sitting in judgment. Chase was acquitted of all charges in a case that many historians credit with ensuring the independence of the judiciary.

Chase was still serving on the court in 1811 when he suffered a heart attack and passed away. He was laid to rest In Baltimore's Old St. Paul's Cemetery. Though the cemetery has been designated as a historic site by the United States government it sits behind a locked fence and is overgrown and neglected. Were Chase alive today he would likely be quite outspoken and leading protests relative to the lack of care being shown to what should be a revered property.

George Clymer
(1739–1813)

A Pennsylvania Patriot

Buried at Friends' Burying Ground.
Trenton, New Jersey.

Declaration of Independence • U.S. Constitution

George Clymer of Pennsylvania was an early proponent of independence from Great Britain. He was one of only five people who signed both the Declaration of Independence and the Constitution. He was a Continental Congressman and a member of the First Congress of the United States in 1789.

Clymer was born in Philadelphia on March 16, 1739, to Christopher Clymer and Deborah (née Fitzwater) Clymer. Christopher was a ship's captain who had emigrated from Bristol, England. He was the son of Richard Clymer of Bristol. Deborah's parents were George Fitzwater and Mary Hardiman, Quakers from Philadelphia. Christopher Clymer died in 1740. Deborah followed a few years later or possibly remarried leaving George an orphan at an early age.

Orphaned George was sent to live with his mother's sister and her husband, Hannah and William Coleman. Coleman was a wealthy merchant who was a leader among the Quakers, also known as the Society of Friends. Coleman saw to Clymer's education and George followed in Coleman's footsteps as a merchant. In his 20s, Clymer worked in Coleman's counting house and with Reese Meredith in 1764. Soon Meredith and Clymer became business partners. Clymer married Reese Meredith's daughter Elizabeth in 1765, further cementing the business arrangements. The couple had nine children, five of whom lived to adulthood.

Portrait of George Clymer by Charles Willson Peale.

George Clymer joined the patriot cause around the time of the Sugar Act (1764) and the Stamp Act (1765). As a leader in the Philadelphia business community, he signed the nonimportation agreement that stymied trade with Britain and led to the repeal of the Stamp Act in 1766.

William Coleman died in 1769, leaving a large inheritance to Clymer. At the age of 39, Clymer was now independently wealthy and entered the political realm. He was elected to Philadelphia's City Council and was later a justice and an alderman. Following the British response to the Boston Tea Party in 1774, Clymer joined Pennsylvania's Committee of Correspondence calling for a meeting in Philadelphia that would become the First Continental Congress. He was named to the Congress and became the Continental Treasurer in July 1775, sharing the duties with Michael Hillegas. In November 1775, Clymer was appointed to the Pennsylvania Committee of Safety which took control of the government of Pennsylvania and saw to its defense.

Some of the initial delegates from Pennsylvania who were asked to sign the Declaration of Independence refused to do so, including John Dickinson, Andrew Allen, Charles Humphreys, and Thomas Willing. On July 20, 1776, Clymer, along with George Ross, Benjamin Rush, George Taylor, and James Wilson, were all elected to the Continental Congress with the express purpose of signing the Declaration. They did so, and though Clymer was late to sign it, "[he] affixed his signature to the manifesto, as if in the performance of an act which was about to consummate his dearest wishes, and realize those fond prospects of national prosperity which had ever been transcendent in his thoughts."

Clymer continued in his service as a Continental Congressman, visiting the army at Ticonderoga in September of 1776, and participating through 1777 and then 1780-1782. During this time, he also was a delegate to Pennsylvania's Constitutional Convention and helped form the Bank of Pennsylvania with Robert Morris. Morris and Clymer were then co-directors of the Bank of North America starting in 1781.

In 1787, Clymer, along with Ben Franklin and James Wilson, was named as Pennsylvania delegates to the Constitutional Convention. George was focused on the financial aspects of the proceedings including the assumption of war debts by the central government. Clymer was a strong proponent for a bicameral legislature. Upon ratification, Clymer was elected to the First Congress (1789-1791) but did not seek a second term.

Back in Pennsylvania, Clymer was the head of the Pennsylvania Department of Excise Taxes. When the Whiskey Rebellion broke out in defiance to whiskey taxes, Meredith Clymer, George's son, was among the military force that put down the insurrection. In a stroke of incredibly bad luck young Clymer was one of the few militiamen killed by the rebels. The elder Clymer was devastated and resigned his post. His last public service was at the end of Washington's second term in 1796 when the first president named Clymer to a panel that negotiated peace with the Creek and Cherokee nations in Georgia. A treaty was completed by the next year.

Through his remaining years, Clymer focused on philanthropic pursuits, raising funds for the University of Pennsylvania and serving as the president of the Pennsylvania Academy of

Fine Arts. He served as president of the Philadelphia Society for Promoting Agriculture from 1805 to 1813. He was also president of the Philadelphia Bank from 1803 until his death.

George Clymer died at his son Henry's home in Morrisville, Pennsylvania, just across the Delaware River from Trenton, New Jersey, on January 23, 1813. He was 73 years old. None of the obituaries mentioned his signing of our nation's most important documents. He was laid to rest at the Friends' Burying Ground in Trenton, New Jersey, despite not being the place where he was born, lived, served, or died. He has a very simple grave that borders a parking lot.

The very modest grave of George Clymer at Friends Burying Ground in Trenton, New Jersey (photo by Lawrence Knorr).

John Collins
(1717–1795)

Rhode Island Representative

Buried at Collins Burial Ground,
Newport, Rhode Island.

Articles of Confederation

John Collins was the third governor of Rhode Island, a Continental Congressman, and a signer of the Articles of Confederation. He is credited with casting the deciding vote in Rhode Island to adopt the U.S. Constitution.

John Collins was born in Newport, Rhode Island, on June 8, 1717, the son of Samuel and Elizabeth Collins. He was a businessman and merchant by trade, selling merchandise in Newport that he had acquired through trade as far away as the Mississippi River. He married Mary Avery, the daughter of John Avery of Boston, and the couple had a son also named John Collins and a daughter Abigail.

During the War of Independence, Collins was sent by Rhode Island to the Continental Congress where he served from 1778 to 1780 and again from 1782 to 1783. Collins was involved in activities regarding the army, navy, and finance.

After the war, Collins was elected Governor of Rhode Island, serving from 1786 to 1790. An article in *The Universal Asylum* magazine from June 1790 related the closeness of Collins and Benjamin Franklin. The article stated:

> John Collins was one of Franklin's most intimate acquaintance. This was a boy who was very fond of reading. With him, Franklin often disputed on various subjects. Like most young disputants, they were very warm and very desirous of consulting each other.

> One subject was started, which produced a longer discussion than usual. It was respecting the propriety of educating the female sex, and their abilities for acquiring knowledge. Collins endeavored to show, that they were naturally unequal to the talk of study and that a learned education was improper for them. Franklin supported the opposite opinion, with much warmth, though he was occasionally staggered, more by the greater fluency of his adversary, than by the strength of his arguments.

After the U.S. Constitution was drafted in Philadelphia in 1787, it was sent to the 13 states to be ratified. Each state had to decide whether or not to hold a state convention and then proceed to vote. Rhode Island lagged the other colonies in approving the Constitution, holding out for a Bill of Rights. During this time, Rhode Island was in effect an independent nation with Collins as its head of state. The state remained deeply divided even after the Bill of Rights was introduced, but Collins called for a vote for a convention anyway. In the end, he was the one to cast the deciding vote that called for a state convention in Rhode Island. Without his vote, Rhode Island would not have adopted the Constitution.

There is no known portrait of John Collins. This image is of the historic Colony House in Newport, Rhode Island, which was the seat of government in colonial times.

The grave of John Collins at the Collins Burial Ground, Newport, Rhode Island (photo by Lawrence Knorr).

Following the ratification of the Constitution, Collins was nominated for a seat in the First Congress, but he refused it even though he was elected. Collins wife, Mary, had died in 1788 at the age of 53. Collins also left the governorship in 1790.

John Collins died in Newport on March 4, 1795, at the age of 78. He was laid to rest in the Collins family burial ground on their Newport, Rhode Island estate, "Brenton Neck." By 1854, the burial ground had become so rundown that relatives restored the graves and stones. In 2002, the Sons of the American Revolution placed a stone next to his cenotaph that reads, "The Hon. John Collins, June 8, 1717-March 8, 1795, was elected to the Continental Congress and Served His Country in that Capacity from 1778-1783. He was Then Elected Rhode Island's 3rd Governor, Further Serving His State and Country in that Capacity from 1786 to 1790. Gov. Collins Cast the Deciding Vote

Calling for an Assembly, Which When Convened Voted for Rhode Island to Enter the Union of States."

Abigail Collins, the daughter of John and Mary, married John Warren, a surgeon in the Continental Army and founder of Harvard Medical School. Warren was the younger brother of Dr. Joseph Warren. Collins' grandson, John Collins Covell (1823-1887) was a principal of the Virginia and West Virginia schools for the deaf and blind. Collins' great-great-grandson, Collins Lawton Balch (1834-1910) was a successful businessman and merchant in Rhode Island.

The Rhode Island Society of the Sons of the American Revolution holds an annual observance of Rhode Island Independence Day every May 4th at Collins' grave.

Francis Dana
(1743–1811)
Congressman at Valley Forge

Buried at Old Burying Ground,
Cambridge, Massachusetts.

Articles of Confederation • Diplomat

Francis Dana was an American statesman, lawyer, and jurist from Massachusetts. He served as a delegate to the Continental Congress in 1777-1778 and again in 1784. He was a signer of the Articles of Confederation.

He was born on June 13, 1743, in Charlestown, Massachusetts. His parents were wealthy and respectable and gave him the benefit of an excellent education. He graduated from Harvard in 1762 and took up the practice of law. He was admitted to the bar and set up a practice in Boston in 1767. He opposed British colonial policy and became a leader of the Sons of Liberty. He was elected to Massachusetts' provincial congress in 1774. In the spring of 1774, the Continental Congress felt it important to send someone to England to represent the patriots and to ascertain the real feeling among England's rulers. Dana was selected. He was just 31 years old. The question was whether we should seek to adjust our differences with England as its colony or whether we should declare absolute independence. He returned in March 1776 convinced that all hope for a friendly settlement must be abandoned. He threw his whole influence for independence. He impressed his convictions upon the Continental Congress and just over three months after his return they voted for Independence.

He was a member of the Massachusetts executive council from 1776 to 1780 and served as a delegate to the Continental Congress from 1776 to 1778. He signed the Articles of Confederation in

Portrait of Francis Dana etched circa 1885.

1778. In January 1778, Congress appointed him chairman of the committee assigned to visit George Washington at Valley Forge and confer with him about the reorganization of the army. The committee spent about three months at Valley Forge and assisted Washington in preparing the plan of reorganization which Congress in the main adopted. In that same year, he was a member of the committee that considered a peace proposal offered by Lord North of Great Britain, which he vigorously opposed and which Congress rejected.

In 1779, France went to war with England and took the side of the colonists. Congress needed to send able and discreet persons to Europe and selected Dana to accompany John Adams and his son John Quincy Adams. In December 1780, Dana was appointed minister resident to the Russian court. He was never officially received at the court of Catherine the Great and left Russia in August 1783. After his return, he was again elected to Congress in 1784. He resigned from Congress 1785 to accept a seat on the Supreme Court of Massachusetts.

Dana was named a delegate to both the Annapolis Convention and the Constitutional Convention but attended neither due to poor health. He was, however, a member of the Massachusetts Ratifying Convention. He left there briefly during its proceedings, after a spat with Elbridge Gerry who opposed the ratification.

Dana was appointed Chief Justice of the Massachusetts Supreme Court in 1791, a position he held until his retirement from the bench in May 1806. He became a charter member of the American Academy of Arts and Sciences in 1780.

Francis Dana died at Cambridge, Massachusetts, on April 25, 1811, and is buried in Cambridge's Old Burying Ground.

The Dana family marker at the Old Burying Ground in Cambridge, Massachusetts (photo by Lawrence Knorr).

William Richardson Davie
(1756–1820)
Hero of Stone Ferry

Buried at Old Waxhaw Presbyterian Church Cemetery,
Lancaster, South Carolina.

Military

Born in England, this Founder served honorably fighting against the British during the Revolutionary War. Even after suffering a serious wound and barely escaping capture, he chose to return to the field of battle after he recovered. After the war, he was elected to the North Carolina House of Commons multiple times. He served as a member of his state's delegation to the 1787 Constitutional Convention. Though he strongly supported the product produced by that gathering, he was not present for the signing ceremony. He argued vigorously for its ratification at the North Carolina state conventions held in 1788 and 1789. He served as governor of North Carolina and as a diplomat on a 1799 peace commission in France. He is considered the Founder of the University of North Carolina. His name was William Richardson Davie.

Davie was born on June 20, 1756, in the village of Egremont, England. His father brought him to the American colonies in 1763. His uncle on his mother's side, the Reverend William Richardson after whom he was named, adopted his nephew and made him his son and heir. When Richardson passed away, Davie inherited 150 acres and a large library. From this point on, he always used his full name as a way to honor his uncle. He was educated locally before attending what is now Princeton University. Among his fellow students at the time were Jonathon Dayton, Gunning Bedford, Jr., and James Madison. If the phrase 'we're getting the

Posthumous portrait of William Richardson Davie, painted by Charles Willson Peale in 1826.

band back together had been in vogue at the time this quartet could have used it prior to the 1787 Constitutional Convention.

After leaving Princeton, Davie applied himself to the study of law until this effort was interrupted by the Revolution. In 1778, he decided to join a militia force commanded by General Allen Jones. Jones directed his force to Charleston, South Carolina with the intention of providing for the defense of the port city against a British attack. When the English threat failed to materialize, the troops returned to North Carolina.

In 1779, Davie raised and trained a cavalry troop. The troop was assigned to serve under General Casimir Pulaski who promoted Davie to the rank of major. On June 20, 1779, Davie led a charge against the British forces during the Battle of Stone Ferry. It was during this engagement that his thigh was seriously wounded and he was thrown from his horse. Fortunate to avoid capture, he spent five months in a Charleston hospital recovering from his injuries.

By 1780 Davie had regained his health and once again formed a company of cavalry. He was ordered to protect the region between Charlotte and Camden and performed the duties so well that he was made colonel commandant of the cavalry of North Carolina.

During this time the British led by General Cornwallis had begun an invasion of the southern states. When the invaders under the command of Colonel Tarleton entered Charlotte, Davie twice led aggressive assaults on the enemy forces despite being heavily outnumbered. When the English forces retreated two weeks later, Davie ordered his men to disrupt their withdrawal through skirmishes with the enemy units.

On August 16, 1780, American forces under the command of General Horatio Gates were soundly defeated in the Battle of Camden. Gates rallied his defeated forces and retreated into North Carolina. Davie didn't move his forces north with Gates. Instead he headed south towards the enemy with the goal of recovering abandoned supply wagons and gathering information on the movement of the British forces. So successful was this endeavor that it cost Davie his field command. General Gates was in desperate need of more provisions and so impressed with Davie that he was appointed to the post of commissary-general. In this position, he oversaw the locating, organizing, and transportation of supplies for the troops under Gates' command.

After the revolution, Davie's prominence in North Carolina grew as both a lawyer and a public speaker. He became involved politically and was elected to the North Carolina House of Commons. In 1787, he was sent to Philadelphia as one of North Carolina's representatives at the Constitutional Convention.

Davie was much involved in resolving one of the major issues facing those at the convention. That question involved the delicate issue of slavery and how the slaves, held largely in the south, would be counted in determining representation in the House of Representatives. Many of the northern delegates objected to the slaves being counted at all. A compromise that would have counted each slave as three-fifths of a free citizen was rejected on July 11th by a vote of six states to four. Every northern state except Connecticut voted against the proposal. South Carolina remained opposed to the compromise as their delegates were insisting that every slave be counted the same as a free person. After the vote, Davie drew a line in the sand saying that North Carolina "would never confederate on any terms that did not rate them [slaves} at least as three-fifths," he then went on to declare that if the south were denied a share of representation for their black slaves then the work of the convention "was at an end."

Davie was among the delegates chosen to serve on a committee to propose a solution to the stalemate. The result was the "Great Compromise." The proposal that resulted was that the three-fifths rule would apply both in apportioning direct taxes and in determining representation in the House. The northern states were attracted to the additional tax revenues and the southern states satisfied by the partial counting of their slaves. The proposal was approved unanimously. In his 1966 book titled *1787: The Grand Convention*, Clinton Rossiter described Davie as "an agent if not an architect of the Great Compromise."

Davie returned to North Carolina before the Constitution was signed but he was a strong advocate for ratification at his state conventions in both 1788 and 1789. He voiced his frustration with those who opposed ratification saying, "It is much easier to alarm people than to inform them."

In 1798, Davie was elected Governor of North Carolina. He resigned the office a year later when President Adams requested that he serve on a peace commission to France. A staunch Federalist, Davie made an unsuccessful run for a seat in the House of Representatives in 1804. During the war of 1812, he

The grave of William Richardson Davie at Old Waxhaw Presbyterian Church Cemetery in Riverside, South Carolina (photo by Lawrence Knorr).

served in the army but declined an offer to be appointed Major General from President Madison. Davie died at his estate in South Carolina on November 29, 1820. He was laid to rest in the Old Waxhaw Presbyterian Church Cemetery.

Davie earned acclaim as a soldier, a politician, and a diplomat but his accomplishments didn't end there. As a member of the North Carolina legislature, he sponsored a bill that chartered the University of North Carolina. He laid the cornerstone of the university in October of 1793 and is recognized as the founder of the institution.

William Henry Drayton
(1742–1779)

Died in Philadelphia

Buried at Christ Church Burial Grounds,
Philadelphia, Pennsylvania.
In 1979, soil from the grave reburied at "Drayton Hall,"
Charleston, South Carolina.

Articles of Confederation

This Founder initially opposed the growing colonial resistance to British rule after the Stamp Act. As a matter of fact he wrote a series of articles defending the actions taken by England. When these articles were published in Europe he was appointed as a member of the Colonial Council in 1772. Over the next two years his views on colonial rule changed drastically and in 1774 he authored a pamphlet titled the *American Claim of Rights* which supported the call for a Continental Congress. As a result he was removed from his government position which only served to strengthen his views on the rebel cause. During the revolution he represented South Carolina in the Continental Congress. As a member of that Congress he signed the Articles of Confederation. He died before reaching the age of forty and before the end of the Revolution. He remains one of our lesser-known Founders. His name was William Henry Drayton.

Drayton was born in the month of September in 1742 at his father's plantation, "Drayton Hall," located on the banks of the Ashley River near Charleston, South Carolina. His birth took place shortly after his father completed construction of the main house located on the large rice plantation. His mother was Charlotta Bull Drayton the daughter of the colony's governor William Bull. His well-connected family sent him to England in 1750 for his education. He attended the Westminster School and Balliol College,

Portrait of William Henry Drayton courtesy of the Library of Congress.

Oxford before returning to America in 1764. Upon his return, he studied law and was admitted to the South Carolina bar.

As mentioned above, Drayton's conversion to the American cause was not complete until the mid-1770s. By 1775, he was a member of South Carolina's Committee of Safety and the provisional Congress that functioned as the rebel government of South Carolina. In 1776, he was appointed to the position of Chief Justice on his state's Supreme Court. That same year Drayton raised two battalions to fight in the war against England. South Carolina sent him to Georgia for the purpose of proposing that Georgia, with its smaller population, would benefit by being annexed to its eastern neighbor. Though the proposal was debated, Georgia rejected the idea. A year later, Drayton appealed directly to the citizens of Georgia attempting to convince them of the advantages of joining South Carolina. This resulted in Georgia's governor offering a reward of 100 pounds for the capture of Drayton. Though he accused the governor of "nonsense and falsehoods," Drayton returned to South Carolina and abandoned the effort to annex the neighboring state.

In 1778, South Carolina sent Drayton to Philadelphia as a representative in the Continental Congress. As a member of Congress, he was a strong supporter of the military and a signer of the Articles of Confederation. Drayton didn't live long enough to see the Articles ratified or the revolution he championed succeed. While serving in Congress he passed away from typhus on September 3, 1779. He was laid to rest in Philadelphia's Christ Church Burial Ground in a now unknown location. In 1979 dust from what was believed to be his grave were taken to "Drayton Hall" in South Carolina.

On September 25, 1779, the *Virginia Gazette* reported Drayton's death. The paper noted that Drayton had been honored by his country through his appointment to the "most important and confidential offices." The report went on to say that at the time of his death he was Chief Justice of his state and one of its representatives in Congress. The paper also proclaimed that Drayton's writings were well-known and studied in both America and Europe. Since he passed away before he reached the age of forty, there is little doubt that had he lived he would have made an even greater mark on the young country he well represented. His past service and reputation would have assured him a voice as the new nation found its footing after the war with England was won.

Plaque honoring William Henry Drayton at Christ Church Burial Ground in Philadelphia, Pennsylvania (photography by Lawrence Knorr).

William Ellery
(1727–1820)
Early Abolitionist

Buried at Common Burying Ground,
Newport, Rhode Island.

Declaration of Independence • Articles of Confederation

This Founder once wrote a letter to one of his grandsons enumerating the jobs he had been employed in over the years. Putting pen to paper he stated, "I have been a clerk of the court, a quack lawyer, a member of Congress, one of the Lords of the Admiralty, a judge, a loan officer, and finally a collector of the customs, and thus, not without many difficulties, but as honestly, thank God, as most men, I have got through the journey of a varied and sometimes anxious life." As part of that journey, he added his signature to the document declaring American independence. His name was William Ellery.

Ellery was born on December 22, 1727, in Newport, Rhode Island. His father was a graduate of Harvard and a wealthy merchant. He was initially educated by his father and eventually also found his way to Harvard from which he graduated at the age of twenty. He then returned to Newport where he first attempted to follow in his father's shoes as a merchant.

Ellery married twice, first in 1750 to Ann Remington who died in 1764 and again in 1767 when he wed Abigail Cary. In the course of these marriages, he fathered at least sixteen children, though some put the number at nineteen. Only one other signer, Carter Braxton, is recorded as fathering more. Needless to say, providing for a family of this size took a lot of his energy, though clearly not all of it.

Portrait of William Ellery, artist unknown.

Ellery, as stated in his aforementioned letter, worked a number of jobs until at age forty he achieved a life's ambition and began to practice law. He was a successful lawyer working in both his home state and nearby Massachusetts. At this same time, he became involved in the political scene becoming active in the Sons of Liberty. Like many of the patriots of his day he strongly opposed the Stamp Act and the Intolerable Acts.

In 1776, Samuel Ward, a former Rhode Island governor who was one of the two Rhode Island representatives to the Continental Congress, died after contracting smallpox. Ellery was the choice to replace him. Thus he arrived in Congress shortly before the Declaration of Independence was adopted and signed. In both the play and the movie *1776* it is the other Rhode Island delegate, Stephen Hopkins, who is portrayed as finding a spot where he could see each man's face as he signed the Declaration. In reality, it was Ellery who did so. Describing the scene he said, "I

Marker honoring William Ellery.

was determined to see how they all looked as they signed what might be their death warrant. I placed myself beside the secretary Charles Thomson and eyed each closely as he affixed his name to the document. Undaunted resolution was displayed on every countenance."

During the Revolution, the British seized Newport and burned Ellery's home to the ground. During the occupation, he and his family fled to Dighton, Massachusetts where they resided until it was safe to return to their home and begin the rebuilding process.

After joining Congress, Ellery would remain a member of that body for eight of the next ten years. In 1922, the *Altoona Tribune* described him as one of its most influential members. During this period, he also signed the Articles of Confederation and served on numerous committees including war wounded, army purchases, and public accounts.

In 1786, Ellery left Congress and returned to Rhode Island to attend to his personal affairs, most notably shoring up his financial situation. He worked a number of jobs until 1790 when President Washington appointed him customs collector for Newport. The appointment solidified him financially and he held the post until his death.

Ellery was one of three signers of the Declaration of Independence who lived into their nineties, dying at the age of

The grave of William Ellery at Common Burying Ground & Island Cemetery in Newport, Rhode Island (photo by Lawrence Knorr).

92 on February 15, 1820. He was laid to rest in the Common Burying Ground in Newport, Rhode Island.

There is an annual commemoration held at his grave every July 4th sponsored by the Sons of the Revolution and the William Ellery Chapter of the Daughters of the American Revolution. A town in New York and an avenue in Middletown, Rhode Island are named in his honor.

Deborah Sampson Gannett
(1760 – 1827)
Female Minuteman

Buried at Rock Ridge Cemetery,
Sharon, Massachusetts.

Military

Deborah Sampson Gannett, more commonly known as Deborah Sampson was a Massachusetts woman who disguised herself as a man to serve in the Continental Army from May 1782 to October 1783, during the American Revolutionary War. She is one of a very small number of women with a documented record of military combat experience in that war. She served for seventeen months in the army under the name of Robert Shurtleff (also spelled Shirtliffe and Shurtliff in various sources). She was wounded in battle in 1782 and honorably discharged at West Point in 1783. She was also one of the first women to receive a pension for military service and the first woman to go on a national lecture tour.

Deborah Sampson was born on December 17, 1760, in Plympton, Massachusetts. She was one of seven children born to Jonathan Sampson and Deborah Bradford. Some of Deborah's ancestors included passengers on the *Mayflower*. One of these, Priscilla Mullins Alden, was later immortalized in Longfellow's poem, "The Courtship of Miles Standish."

Jonathan abandoned his family and took up with a woman named Martha in Lincoln County, Maine. Her mother was in poor health and could not provide for the children so they were placed with friends and relatives. Deborah, at the age of five, was sent to live with an elderly widow Mary Thatcher. Upon the death of the widow when Deborah was eight, she became an indentured

Portrait of Deborah Sampson Gannett, artist unknown.

servant in the household of Jeremiah Thomas in Middleborough, Massachusetts. Mr. Thomas had ten sons and as an indentured servant she was bound to serve the family until she was eighteen. She was given food, clothing, and shelter in exchange. She was, however, not sent to school like the Thomas boys because Mr. Thomas did not believe in education for women. She learned by having the Thomas boys review their studies with her each night after her chores were done. She grew to be approximately 5'9" tall when the average at that time was 5' for a woman and 5'6" to 5'8" for a man.

When she turned eighteen, she was released from her indentured servitude and took a job as a schoolteacher. She supplemented her income by spinning and weaving at various homes and at Sproat Tavern, a gathering place for men who discussed the battles of the revolution.

In early 1782, Sampson wore men's clothing and joined an Army unit in Middleborough under the name of Timothy Thayer. She collected a bonus but failed to show up at the appointed time. She had been recognized by a local resident. She paid back a portion of the bonus she hadn't spent and the Army did not punish her. She tried it again in the town of Uxbridge, Massachusetts near Worcester on May 20, 1782, and this time was successful. She used the name Robert Shurtleff and was chosen for the Light Infantry Company of the 4th Massachusetts Regiment. Light infantry companies were elite troops, specially picked because they were taller and stronger than average. They were referred to as "light" infantry because they travelled with less equipment and supplies and took part in small, risky missions.

Her regiment marched from Worcester to West Point to protect the Hudson Highlands from the British who still occupied New York City. There were numerous skirmishes between the two forces along "no man's land." At one point, Sampson's regiment encountered another American unit headed by Colonel Ebenezer Sproat. She had spent time working at Sproat Tavern owned by the Colonel's father, and feared she would be recognized but was not.

During her first major battle, on July 3, 1782, near Tarrytown, New York she received two musket balls in her thigh and a slash in her forehead from a sabre. She begged her fellow soldiers to leave her alone and let her die, but they refused, put her on a horse, and rode six miles to a hospital. When she arrived, doctors treated her head wound but Deborah did not tell them about her thigh wounds fearful that they would discover her true sex. She limped out of the hospital and removed one of the balls with a penknife and a sewing needle. The second ball was too deep for her to reach. Her leg never fully healed and bothered her for the rest of her life.

She was some time recovering from her wounds before she could rejoin her company. On April 1, 1783, Sampson was promoted and spent seven months serving as a personal orderly to General John Patterson. In June, the Fourth Massachusetts was transferred to Philadelphia. That summer she became ill with a severe fever, rendering her unconscious. She was cared for by Dr. Barnabus Binney who discovered that Robert Shurtleff was really a woman. He did not reveal his discovery but took her to his house where his wife and daughters and a nurse took care of her.

When she recovered, Dr. Binney asked Deborah to deliver a note to General Patterson. She correctly assumed it would reveal her gender. Patterson notified General Henry Knox who in turn notified General Washington. He ordered her honorably discharged. She received her honorable discharge on October 25, 1783, at West Point after a year and a half of service.

Sampson returned home and on April 7, 1785, married Benjamin Gannett, a farmer from Sharon, Massachusetts. They had three children and adopted one. Life was hard for the Gannetts as the farm was small and the land was not productive because it had been worked extensively.

In 1792, Sampson petitioned the Massachusetts State Legislature for pay that had been withheld because she was a woman. The legislature granted her thirty-four pounds with

Bronze statue of Deborah Sampson Gannett in front of the public library in Sharon, Massachusetts (photo by Lawrence Knorr).

interest back to her discharge date. The order was signed by Governor John Hancock. At the urging of her friend Paul Revere, Sampson went on tour in 1802, capitalizing on her wartime fame. She lectured in Massachusetts, Rhode Island, and New York and was perhaps America's first woman lecturer. She delivered a set of speeches about her wartime experiences and at the conclusion of her speech, she would leave the stage and return in uniform and demonstrate how to clean, load, and fire a musket. Her audiences were astonished.

The grave of Deborah Sampson Gannett (photo by Lawrence Knorr).

In 1804, she petitioned Congress for a pension for her wartime service. Paul Revere wrote a letter in support of her petition. This had never before been requested by or for a woman. On March 11, 1805, Congress approved the request and placed her on the Massachusetts Invalid Pension Roll at the rate of four dollars a month. In 1816, Congress increased her pension to $6.40 a month.

In 1813, Sampson moved in with her son and daughter-in-law in Sharon and died there on April 29, 1827, at the age of 66. She was buried in nearby Rock Ridge Cemetery. Her gravestone is located a short distance from the hill on which her grandson, George Washington Gay, erected a monument to her and the Civil War veterans many years later.

The town of Sharon memorializes Sampson with Deborah Sampson Street, a statue in front of the public library, Deborah Sampson Field, and the Deborah Sampson House which is privately owned and not open to the public.

The town of Plympton, Massachusetts has a boulder on the town green with a bronze plaque inscribed to Sampson's memory.

In 1983, Governor Michael Dukakis signed a proclamation which declared Deborah Sampson as the Official Heroine of the Commonwealth of Massachusetts.

Horatio Gates
(1727–1806)
Hero of Saratoga

Buried at Trinity Church Graveyard,
New York, New York.

Military

Horatio Lloyd Gates was a retired major in the British army who was acquainted with George Washington from as early as the ill-fated Braddock Expedition during the French and Indian War. At the outset of the American Revolution, he visited Washington at "Mount Vernon" and asked to serve in the Continental Army. Washington urged Congress to appoint him and he proved to be one of the most controversial figures in American military history.

Gates was born July 26, 1727, in Maldon, England, the son of Robert and Dorothea Gates. Due to his family's status, he obtained a military commission in 1745, serving with the 20th Foot in Germany during the War of the Austrian Succession. Following his service in Europe, he came to America at age twenty-two in the company of Edward Cornwallis, the then governor of Nova Scotia and uncle of General Charles Cornwallis. By 1754, he was promoted to captain in the 45th Foot and saw action in battles there, especially at Chignecto. He married his wife Elizabeth that year in Halifax and sold his commission to purchase a captaincy in New York.

During the French and Indian War, Gates served under General Edward Braddock in America. In early July 1755, General Braddock sent a small contingent led by Captain Gates ahead of his army that was cutting a road through the wilderness to Fort Duquesne in western Pennsylvania. Braddock was making no secret of his advance and both the occupants of the fort and

Portrait of Horatio Gates, circa 1794, by Gilbert Stuart.

the local natives were well-aware of his army. Gates secured the two Monongahela River crossings without incident. After crossing 300 yards of shallow river at the second site, Gates awaited the progress of the main column about seven hours later. They arrived marching boldly with flags unfurled and the band playing "Grenadiers' March."

Captain Beaujeu, at the fort, immediately sent his force of soldiers and native warriors into the woods around the front of Braddock's men. Using the trees for cover, the French and Indians began firing, halting the advance of the British who began returning fire in a disciplined manner. Soon, the Canadian militia and French regulars were turned back, their captain dead, but the Indians remained firing at anything in the open. Gates opened fire on the Indians with his small cannons but was thwarted by their sudden movements through the trees.

Braddock rode forward to the front of the collapsing column just when the Americans had abandoned the ranks and went to fighting Indian-style in the trees. The British stood their position in the open, firing at the natives and sometimes hitting the friendly American militia. The Indians focused their fire primarily on the officers with great result, leaving the foot soldiers with no one to give them orders. Gates received a severe bullet wound and had to give up his cannons, his men falling in with the regulars who were running out of ammunition and were scrounging for cartridges from their fallen compatriots.

Aide de camp George Washington, who had been suffering terribly from dysentery, charged into the midst, attempting to rally the men. In his report, he recorded twelve musket balls pierced his coat, but not his flesh—an example of the incredible luck he had in combat. After three hours of battle, Braddock's horse was shot out from under him. While trying to mount another, he was mortally wounded in the arm and lung. With Washington's help, Braddock was carried to the rear. The men turned and ran, some throwing their muskets to run as fast as possible. Many were shot from behind by the pursuing Indians.

When the Indians paused to scalp and plunder, Washington organized the fleeing British troops into a rear guard and then ordered the main body to bring forward medical supplies and wagons to move the wounded. The British lost 83 of 89 officers killed or wounded and nearly 900 of the 1466 men in the army. The other side lost less than 100 killed or wounded.

A few days later, as the British retreated down the road they had hacked through the wilderness, Braddock succumbed to his wounds. He was buried in the middle of the road. The wagons then rode over the grave to conceal it from the Indians. Gates made it back thanks to Washington's courage and quick action.

Elizabeth Gates gave birth to their son Robert in 1758. Meanwhile, Gates served as a major under General Monckton during the capture of Martinique in 1762. As the war ended, Gates' opportunity for advancement disappeared. Frustrated, he sold his major's commission in England and returned to North America. In 1772, he reconnected with George Washington and settled on a modest plantation near Shepherdstown in Berkeley County, Virginia (now West Virginia).

As the Revolutionary War was commencing in May 1775, Gates went to "Mount Vernon" and offered his service to Washington.

Congress then appointed Gates Brigadier General and the first Adjutant General of the Continental Army. In this role, he created the army's system of records and orders and helped to standardize the regiments from various colonies. During the siege of Boston, he was a voice of caution.

Longing for field command, in June 1776 he was promoted to Major General and given command of the Canadian Department, replacing John Sullivan, whose army was in disarray as it retreated from Quebec. By summer, his army had regrouped at Fort Ticonderoga, where he was in command of the defense of Lake Champlain. General Schuyler took over command of the Canadian Department. Gates spent the summer preparing the American fleet on the lake for defense. Benedict Arnold, an experienced seaman, was his key subordinate. Arnold then sailed to face the British in the Battle of Valcour Island in October. Though a defeat, it delayed the British advance on Ticonderoga until the following year.

With additional time bought, Gates marched some of his army south to meet up with Washington in Pennsylvania following the fall of New York City. When Washington decided to attack Trenton, Gates advised further retreat and then did so himself, leaving his men behind. Claiming illness, he headed to Baltimore to meet with the Continental Congress where he discussed his desire to take charge of the army in place of Washington. Meanwhile, Washington produced stunning victories at Trenton and Princeton, eliminating doubts about his ability.

Gates was sent back to the Northern Department but escaped blame for the fall of Ticonderoga in 1777, though he had been in command there for some time. Instead, Schuyler and St. Clair were criticized and Gates was given command of the whole department on August 4, 1777. At the Battles of Saratoga, Gates led the army to victory over General Burgoyne. However, the military action was mostly led by his subordinates including Benedict Arnold, Benjamin Lincoln, Enoch Poor, and Daniel Morgan. Arnold even took the field against Gates' orders to rally the troops in a ferocious attack. Over 5700 British troops surrendered. For this, Congress presented Gates with a gold medal. After the victory, Gates proposed invading Quebec, but Washington rejected the idea. Meanwhile, the French were now convinced to form an alliance against Great Britain in 1778.

Tensions between Washington and Gates were high as Gates tried to leverage political advantage from his victory. He insulted Washington by sending his reports directly to Congress and did not return troops to Washington that were sent to aid him. Gates' friends in Congress appointed him President of the Board of War, the civilian head of the military, making him Washington's superior despite his lower rank. Some members of Congress considered appointing Gates in place of Washington. General Conway made critical remarks about Washington in a letter to Gates. Gates' adjutant, General James Wilkinson, forwarded the letter to General William Alexander, who forwarded it to Washington. What was known as the Conway Cabal came to an end thanks to Congress ending the controversy by endorsing Washington. Gates resigned from the Board of War, apologized to Washington, and took a position in the Eastern Department in November 1778.

In May 1780, after the fall of Charleston, South Carolina and the capture of General Benjamin Lincoln's southern army, Congress voted to place Gates in charge of the Southern Department. He learned of this at home at his plantation and headed south to meet the remaining army near the Deep River in North Carolina in late July. He gathered his forces and marched south to face General Charles Cornwallis, the nephew of his mentor, at Camden, South Carolina. On August 16, his army was routed. Nearly 1000 men were captured along with the army's supplies and artillery. The most noteworthy aspect of the engagement was Gates' personal retreat on horseback of 170 miles in only three days—leaving his army behind. In October, he further learned of his son Robert's demise in combat.

Gates' reputation ruined, he returned home while Nathanael Greene took command of the Southern Department on December 3. Congress called for a board of inquiry, a step before a court-martial. He vehemently opposed such criticism. While never placed in field command again, his friends in Congress repealed the inquiry in 1782. Gates then joined Washington's staff in Newburgh, New York where there were rumblings of a military coup due to the lack of fulfilled promises to the troops. Gates' subordinate, General Armstrong, was found to be organizing action against Congress. It is not clear if Gates was involved in the Newburgh Conspiracy, which was put down by Washington's appeal to the troops and to Congress.

Marker honoring Horatio Gates installed by the Daughters of the American Revolution at Trinity Church Cemetery in New York City.

Elizabeth Gates passed in the summer of 1783. Gates retired a widower to his estate, “Traveler’s Rest” near present-day Kearneysville, Jefferson County, West Virginia. He served as vice president of the Society of the Cincinnati and president of the Virginia chapter. He attempted to marry Janet Montgomery, the widow of General Richard Montgomery, but she rebuffed him. In 1786 he married Mary Valens, a recent immigrant from England who was involved in a boarding school in Maryland. Gates sold his plantation in 1790 and freed his slaves at the urging of his friend John Adams. The aging couple then retired to an estate on Manhattan Island. Gates was elected to a single term in the New York legislature in 1800. He died on April 10, 1806, and was buried in the Trinity Church graveyard on Wall Street in New York City. His actual gravesite within the cemetery is not known but a cenotaph is placed there in his memory.

The town of Gates in Monroe County, New York is named in his honor as are several streets about New York City. In York, Pennsylvania, the General Horatio Gates House was his home during the Second Continental Congress.

Elbridge Gerry
(1744–1814)

Founder of Gerrymandering

Buried at Congressional Cemetery,
Washington, D.C.

Declaration of Independence • Articles of Confederation

Elbridge Gerry was a very important Founder of the United States. He signed the Articles of Confederation and the Declaration of Independence. He was a major figure at the Constitutional Convention speaking to the convention 153 times. He served as Governor of Massachusetts and as Vice President under James Madison. He was smart, well educated, hardworking, and tenacious. He was also regarded as annoying and not well-liked. He would, after addressing the convention 153 times and winning many debates and forcing many compromises, be one of only three men who attended the convention to refuse to sign the Constitution. He then went on to oppose ratification. The term "gerrymandering" was coined while he was governor of Massachusetts and approved a controversial redistricting plan that favored Republicans.

Gerry was born in 1744 at Marblehead, Massachusetts. He was the third of eleven children although only five survived to adulthood. The family was wealthy and Gerry was educated by tutors and entered Harvard just before turning fourteen. After receiving a B.A. in 1762 and an M.A. in 1765, he participated in his father's merchant business. He entered the colonial legislature in 1772 where he worked closely with Samuel Adams. He, Adams, and Hancock served on the Council of Safety where Gerry raised troops and dealt with military logistics. On April 18, 1775, Gerry attended a council meeting at an inn between Lexington

Portrait of Elbridge Gerry by James Bogle after John Vanderlyn.

and Concord and barely escaped the British troops marching on those towns.

In 1774 he was elected to the First Continental Congress but refused to serve because he was grieving the recent loss of his father. In 1776 he served in the Second Continental Congress where he supported and signed the Declaration of Independence and later was a signer of the Articles of Confederation.

Well known for his personal integrity, Gerry felt strongly about and advocated regularly about limiting central government and civilian control of the military. He also opposed the idea of political parties. He felt so strongly about the issue of centralizing too much power that he resigned from the Continental Congress in protest in 1780. He rejoined Congress in 1783 and served until 1785. The next year he married Ann Thompson who was twenty years younger than him. James Monroe was his best man. The couple settled in Cambridge and had ten children between 1787 and 1801.

Gerry played a major role at the U.S. Constitutional Convention held in Philadelphia during the summer of 1787. He arrived in late May several weeks after it had begun. During June he frequently helped check the nationalists by arguing and voting against their motions. He forced them to give up on an absolute veto power for the chief executive and on giving the central government an absolute power to negate state laws.

Gerry advocated indirect elections believing people could be easily misled. He managed to obtain such elections for the Senate whose members were to be elected by state legislatures but was unsuccessful in the case of the House. He made numerous proposals for the indirect election of the chief executive which was somewhat achieved with the Electoral College.

By the end of June, the Convention was on the verge of collapse over the issue of the relationship of the central government to the states. On July 2, after a deadlocked vote on whether the states would be equally represented in the Senate, Gerry told his colleagues that if the Convention failed "we shall not only disappoint America but the rest of the world." A committee was appointed to produce a compromise and Gerry was appointed its chairman. A compromise on the issues was finally achieved which provided for proportional representation in the House and equal representation in the Senate and provided that the House would raise revenue and appropriate money. When Gerry presented the committee report to the full convention for approval he stated: "If we do not come to some agreement among ourselves, some foreign sword will probably do the work for us." On July 15, after ten more days of debate, it was put to a vote. It passed by a 5-4 margin. Gerry had played an important role at a critical juncture in the convention.

Once the convention moved on, Gerry was a strong advocate for issues he believed in. Between July 17 and July 26, he made twenty-nine speeches on the powers to be granted to the central government, the jurisdiction of the judiciary, and the election of the President. He opposed the Congress electing the President instead proposing that the governors select the electors who would elect the President. It was at his urging that the Convention adopted an impeachment provision. He was also successful in proposing that senators of a state vote as individuals rather than cast a single vote on behalf of the state which at that point was the assumption.

During the next six weeks, Gerry made seventy-eight speeches on such issues as limiting the power of the central government, preventing a peacetime standing army, limiting the size of the army, and empowering the President only to make war but not to declare war. He opposed having a Vice President, an office he would one day hold.

Gerry was unhappy about the lack of expression of any sort of individual liberties in the proposed Constitution. On September

The grave of Elbridge Gerry at Congressional Cemetery in Washington, D.C. (photo by Lawrence Knorr).

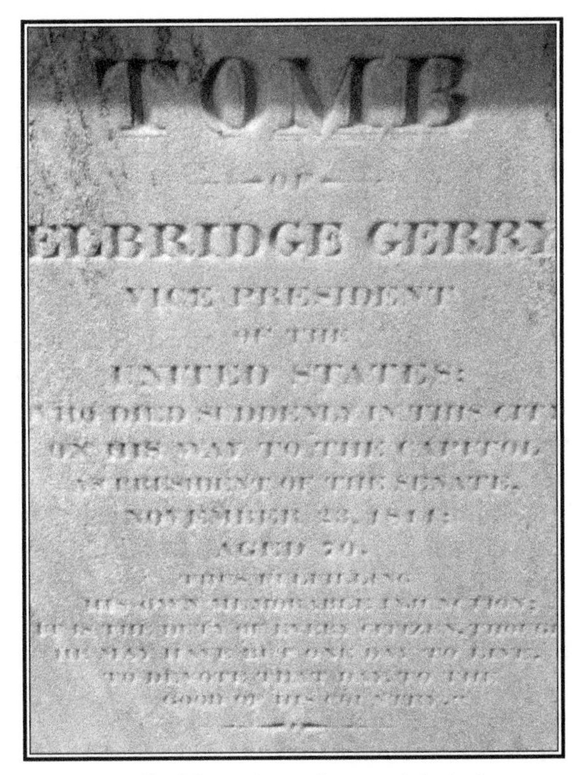

Detail of Gerry's tombstone (photo by Lawrence Knorr).

17, he addressed the Convention for the one hundred fifty-third and last time stating he could not sign the document. He then watched as thirty-nine men signed it. Two others, Edmund Randolph and George Mason, also refused.

Gerry continued his opposition during the ratification debates that took place after the convention. He published a letter that was widely circulated documenting his objections. He cited the lack of a Bill of Rights as his primary objection. If the people adopted the document as it stood, they were in danger of losing their liberties. But if they rejected it altogether, anarchy may ensue. His opposition cost him a number of close political friends. Massachusetts ratified the Constitution but recommended amendments. Before the Massachusetts ratification convention, none of the states had requested amendments. After it, all but one ratified it with proposed amendments.

In 1789, after he announced his intention to support the Constitution, he was elected to the first Congress where he championed federalist policies. He proposed that Congress consider all the proposed constitutional amendments that various states had called for. He successfully lobbied for inclusion of freedom of assembly in the First Amendment and was a leading architect of the Fourth Amendment protections against search and seizure.

In 1793, after two terms in Congress, Gerry did not stand for re-election and returned home. His retirement from public service didn't last long as in 1797 President Adams appointed him to be a member of a special diplomatic commission sent to France to negotiate a reconciliation in hopes of avoiding a war. This episode became known as the XYZ Affair. The mission failed and Gerry's reputation was damaged.

Between 1800 and 1803 Gerry ran four times for the governorship of Massachusetts and lost each time. He tried again in 1810 and won. He repeated a victory in 1811. Both times he ran as a Republican. Near the end of his second term, the Republicans passed a redistricting measure to ensure their domination of the state senate. This led to Federalists heaping ridicule on Gerry and they used the term "gerrymander" to describe the salamander shape of one of the new districts.

He was chosen to be James Madison's vice presidential running mate in 1812 and they easily won. On November 23, 1814, the seventy-year-old Gerry collapsed on his way to the Senate and died. He is buried in the Congressional Cemetery in Washington, D.C. He is depicted in two paintings, the "Declaration of Independence" and "General George Washington Resigning His Commission" both on view in the rotunda of the United States Capitol. He is also depicted in murals in the National Archives near displays of the Articles of Confederation, Declaration of Independence, Constitution, and Bill of Rights.

Nicholas Gilman
(1755–1814)

Soldier and Congressman

Buried at Exeter Cemetery,
Exeter, New Hampshire.

U.S. Constitution • Military

On July 15, 2018, the authors traveled to Exeter, New Hampshire to attend the monument dedication ceremony honoring a Founder organized by his descendants. This patriot made a name for himself at the young age of 21 in his service in the Continental Army. After the Revolution, he represented New Hampshire in the Continental Congress. He was a delegate to the Constitutional Convention and the youngest signer of the document produced by that gathering. He later represented his state in both the House of Representatives and the United States Senate. A true soldier-statesman, his name was Nicholas Gilman.

Gilman was born on August 3, 1755, in Exeter, New Hampshire. He was named after his father who was a shipbuilder and a politician. As a boy, he attended local public schools though it appears his education was limited. He went to work as a clerk in his father's trading house while his older brother John worked in the family's shipbuilding business. The taxes the English imposed on the colonies adversely affected these businesses. Soon after the shooting started at Lexington and Concord, Gilman volunteered to serve in the New Hampshire regiment of the Continental Army, serving in the Third New Hampshire Regiment under its commander Colonel Alexander Scammell.

In 1777 British forces under the command of General John Burgoyne were advancing from Canada and heading to New York. Gilman's regiment marched to Fort Ticonderoga to join other

Portrait of Nicholas Gilman etched by Albert Rosenthal, 1888, based on a miniature in possession of the family.

American forces in halting the British invasion. Burgoyne's experienced regulars proved too much for the American forces and Gilman with his regiment was forced to retreat to avoid capture. It was during this retreat that the American forces utilized delaying tactics to slow the British advance. Meanwhile, Gilman busied himself with the task of supervising the training of the men in his regiment. He and his men participated in two important battles at Freeman's Farm where they inflicted significant damage on the British forces. Though the Americans failed to drive Burgoyne's army from the field of battle, the English lost twice as many men. Eventually, Burgoyne was forced to surrender to the American forces under General Horatio Gates at Saratoga.

After the battle, Scammel led his troops to Philadelphia to reinforce the forces serving under General Washington. Gilman and his unit endured the harsh winter at Valley Forge. Washington selected Colonel Scammell to serve as the Continental Army's Adjutant General and Scammell made Gilman his assistant. In 1778 Gilman was promoted to the rank of captain. Gilman would see action with Washington's army for the remainder of the revolution including the decisive Battle of Yorktown. In the latter part of 1783, Gilman's father passed away and he retired from the army to return home to Exeter to run the family business.

In 1786 the New Hampshire legislature appointed Gilman to serve in the Continental Congress. This appointment, as well as his selection to represent his state at the Annapolis Convention, demonstrated that Gilman's history of service and organizational skills had made him a national leader. As such he was committed to changing the Articles of Confederation which had proven to be ineffective in bringing the states together as a nation.

New Hampshire Senator Maggie Hassan speaking at the dedication of the new grave marker for Nicholas Gilman at Exeter Cemetery in Exeter, New Hampshire on July 15, 2018 (photo by Lawrence Knorr).

Saluting the new grave stone after placing a new Sons of the American Revolution marker (photo by Lawrence Knorr).

In 1787 Gilman represented New Hampshire at the Constitutional Convention in Philadelphia. Coming from one of the smaller states, he championed compromises that gave those states equal representation in the United States Senate with the larger states in the union. After signing the Constitution produced by the Philadelphia Convention, he worked with his brother John to ensure that New Hampshire ratified the government proposed in the document. It is not overstating the facts to say that the influence of the Gilman brothers was a key to the ratification of the Constitution in the Granite State by the narrow vote of 57-47.

Gilman's public service was far from at an end. In 1789 when the first Congress of the United States met in New York, Gilman was there as a member of the House of Representatives. He would serve as a member of Congress for four terms. It was during this period that Gilman demonstrated his capacity for growth and change. He had been a Federalist in supporting the establishment of the stronger federal government that the Constitution provided. With that battle won, he became concerned with the necessity of protecting the common man from potential abuses of the government. He increasingly began siding with the Democratic-Republican party that was headed by Thomas Jefferson. When Jefferson was elected president, he appointed Gilman to the position of a federal bankruptcy commissioner.

In 1804 Gilman was elected to the United States Senate. As a senator, he voted against war with Britain in 1812. In 1814 he was returning home to New Hampshire during a Senate recess when he passed away in Philadelphia. He served his country until the day he took his last breath.

Gilman should be remembered for his belief in and strong support for a strong national government. Indeed he believed such a government was necessary for the nation to survive. On

Detail from Nicholas Gilman's new stone at Exeter Cemetery in Exeter, New Hampshire (photo by Lawrence Knorr).

the day after he signed the Constitution, he said that its adoption or rejection would determine "whether we shall become a respectable nation, or a people torn to pieces . . . and rendered contemptible for ages."

As mentioned previously, the authors attended the monument dedication ceremony honoring Nicholas Gilman held in July of 2018. The ceremony was both moving and appropriate. The guest speakers included two of Gilman's descendants, Mark Gilman and Quentin Gilman. One of Gilman's successors in the United States Senate, Maggie Hassan, also offered comments on Gilman's contributions as a Founding Father. The ceremony could easily serve as a model for honoring other Founders whose contributions have been ignored or forgotten for far too long.

Nathanael Greene
(1742–1786)
Liberator of the South

Buried at Johnson Square,
Savannah, Georgia.

Military

Nathanael Greene, a native of Rhode Island, was a major general during the American Revolution. He was one of three men, besides George Washington and Henry Knox, to serve the entire duration of the war. Greene was second in command to only Washington, and towards the end of the war turned the tide in the British-ravaged south.

Nathanael Greene was born on "Forge Farm" in Potowomut, Rhode Island, on August 7, 1742. He was the son of Nathanael Greene (1707-1768), a Quaker farmer and smith. He was descended from John Greene Sr. and Samuel Gorton who were both early settlers of Warwick, Rhode Island. His mother was Mary Mott, the second wife of Nathanael senior. Greene was mostly self-educated and influenced by Reverend Ezra Stiles, who was later a president of Yale University.

Around the time of his father's death, Greene moved to Coventry, Rhode Island and took charge of the family's foundry. There he also established a public school and was chosen to the Rhode Island Assembly, to which he was re-elected several times. He married Catharine Littlefield in July 1774 with whom he had six children who survived infancy.

Though a Quaker, he eschewed that faith's commitment to pacifism in the face of American independence. In August 1774, Greene helped organize a local militia and began reading extensively about military tactics. In December, he was on a committee

Original portrait of Nathanael Greene painted from life in 1783 by Charles Willson Peale.

to revise militia laws. This focus on the military led to his expulsion from the Quakers.

On May 8, 1775, Greene was promoted to major general of the Rhode Island Army of Observation that formed in response to the siege of Boston. The Continental Congress appointed him a brigadier general in the Continental Army the following month. Washington assigned Greene to command the city of Boston after it was evacuated by the British in March 1776.

On August 9, 1776, Greene was promoted to major general and was given command of the Continental Army on Long Island. He led the construction of entrenchments and fortifications but was prevented by illness from taking part in the Battle of Long Island. Greene advocated for a retreat from New York City and was then stationed on the New Jersey side of the Hudson. After the Americans retreated, Greene commanded one of the two

Equestrian statue of Nathanael Greene at Guilford Court House Battlefield (photo by Lawrence Knorr).

columns at the Battle of Trenton. He urged to press immediately on to Princeton but was rebuffed by his peers.

During the Philadelphia campaign, at the Battle of Brandywine, Greene commanded the reserves. At Germantown, his troops distinguished themselves but were late to the field. In March of 1778, Washington appointed him Quartermaster General at Valley Forge with the understanding he would retain command of troops in the field. Greene was in command of the right wing at Monmouth in late June of 1778.

In August of 1778, Greene returned to his home state of Rhode Island with Lafayette to command the land forces in cooperation with French Admiral d'Estaing at the successful Battle of Rhode Island. Back in New Jersey in June of 1780, Greene was in command at the Battle of Springfield, putting an end to British ambitions in the north. In August, he resigned as Quartermaster General after a long dispute with Congress regarding how the army should be administered and supplied. Washington appointed Greene commander at West Point where he presided over the condemnation of Major John André on September 29, 1780.

On October 5, 1780, Washington appointed Greene as commander of the southern theater, giving him charge of all troops from Delaware to Georgia. He took command at Hillsborough, North Carolina, on December 3, 1780, replacing Horatio Gates.

Greene decided to divide his troops in the face of a superior force under Cornwallis. At Kings Mountain in 1780, Colonel William Campbell captured or killed the entire British force. At Cowpens, on January 17, 1781, General Daniel Morgan captured or killed 90% of the British forces. With over 800 prisoners in tow, the Americans began a strategic retreat to draw Cornwallis out, leveraging light cavalry to harass the enemy. The force successfully crossed the Dan River ahead of the British and reached safety in Virginia. Some have referred to this one of the most masterful military achievements of all time.

Now strengthened by reinforcements, Greene's army re-crossed the Dan River and faced Cornwallis at the Battle of Guilford Court House on ground chosen by Greene. As the Americans were turning the British flank, Cornwallis ordered the cannons to fire on his own troops and the Americans. This repulsed the attack, though Cornwallis lost as many of his own as his enemy. Greene then ordered a tactical retreat that further battered and exhausted Cornwallis. The British withdrew towards Wilmington, North Carolina, while Greene now turned towards the liberation of the low country of South Carolina, achieved by June 1781. After the Battle of Eutaw Springs, the British were now forced to the coast where Greene eventually pinned them at Charleston until the end of the war.

Regarding the Southern Campaign, though defeated in every pitched battle by a superior enemy, Greene managed to divide, elude, and tire his opponent through long marches. The Americans chipped away at a British force that was not being reinforced. Others in the campaign were Polish engineer Tadeusz Kościuszko, cavalry officers Henry ("Light-Horse Harry") Lee and William Washington, and partisan leaders Thomas Sumter, Andrew Pickens, Elijah Clarke, and Francis Marion. In the end, Greene had liberated the southern states from British control. When the Treaty of Paris ended the war, British forces controlled a couple of southern coastal cities, but Greene controlled the rest.

After the war, Greene was an original member of the Rhode Island Society of the Cincinnati, serving as president until his death. Several of the southern states granted him lands and money. He sold most of the land to pay war debts associated with his role as Quartermaster General. He kept the "Mulberry Grove" plantation granted to him near Savannah, Georgia. He was offered the post of Secretary of War by President Washington but declined.

Greene died at "Mulberry Grove" on June 19, 1786, at the age of only 43. He was initially interred at the Graham Vault in Colonial Park Cemetery in Savannah. On October 14, 1902, his remains were moved to a monument in Johnson Square in Savannah.

There are many memorials to Nathanael Greene:

- There are many cities, counties, and parks named after him across the country.
- Ships: four Coast Guard cutters, a James Madison-class nuclear submarine, an Army cargo ship, a Liberty class steam merchant, and a 128-foot Army tug which is still in service today.
- A large portrait hangs in the Rhode Island State House, and a statue stands outside the building.
- A cenotaph to him stands in the Old Forge Burial Ground in Warwick.
- His statue, with that of Roger Williams, represents the state of Rhode Island in the National Hall of Statuary in the Capitol.

Grave of Nathanael Greene beneath Johnson Square in Savannah, Georgia (photo by Joe Farrell).

- In Washington, there is a bronze equestrian statue by Henry Kirke Brown at the center of Stanton Park.
- A small statue by Lewis Iselin, Jr. is outside the Philadelphia Museum of Art.
- An equestrian statue designed by Francis H. Packer at the site of the Battle of Guilford Courthouse.
- A statue stands in the middle of the traffic circle between Greene Street and McGee Street in downtown Greensboro.
- Greeneville, Tennessee and Greene County, Tennessee are named after him.
- The city of Greenville, South Carolina, also named for him, unveiled a statue designed by T. J. Dixon and James Nelson at the corner of South Main and Broad Streets.
- A bronze statue of Greene by sculptor Chas Fagan is in St. Clair Park, in Greensburg, Pennsylvania.
- A statue is in Valley Forge National Military Park, Pennsylvania.
- The Nathanael Greene Homestead is in Coventry, Rhode Island.

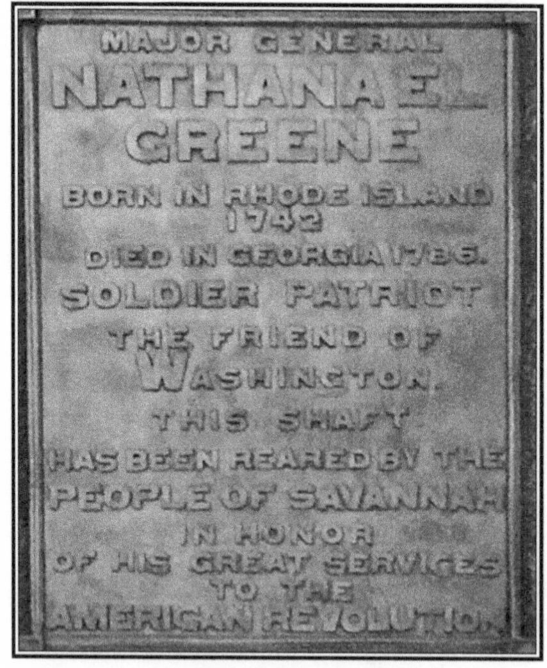

Detail from Nathanael Greene's monument (photo by Joe Farrell).

Button Gwinnett
(1735–1777)
Most Valuable Signature

Buried at Colonial Park Cemetery,
Savannah, Georgia.

Declaration of Independence

The story of Button Gwinnett is unusual. He was born in England where he failed as a merchant. He came to America for what seemed a better opportunity and a fresh start but he failed as a merchant in Charleston and then again in Savannah. He bought land in Georgia and tried life as a planter but this too failed. A late convert to the independence cause, he was elected to the Continental Congress in 1776, signed the Declaration of Independence, and was killed in a duel with a political rival shortly thereafter at the age of forty-five.

Button Gwinnett was born in Gloucestershire County to a Welsh father and an English mother. There are conflicting reports on the exact date of his birth but he was baptized on April 10, 1735, in St. Catherine's Church in Gloucester. Not much is known of his formal education, but he was apprenticed to a merchant in the city of Bristol. He married Ann Bourne in 1757. He was the sole owner of the brig *Nancy*, but his business proved unsuccessful and his ship was seized and sold to pay his debts. Seeking opportunity, he and his family set out for America arriving in Charleston in 1765. He set himself up as a trader but after a few years he sold all his merchandise and moved to Savannah where he opened a store. This venture also failed and he bought a large tract of land on St. Catherine's Island and became a planter.

Around this time, Gwinnett befriended Lyman Hall, a future signer of the Declaration, who had re-settled in Georgia from New

Portrait of Button Gwinnett by Nathaniel Hone the Elder.

England. Through his friendship with Hall, Gwinnett developed an interest in politics and in 1769 was elected to the Georgia Colonial Assembly. More financial problems limited his involvement in public service over the next few years. In 1772, he acquired property in St. John's Parish but in 1773 creditors seized his properties. He was allowed to continue living in his home there for the rest of his life.

Prior to 1775, Gwinnett was known to be a patriotic citizen but he felt successful resistance to so mighty a power as that of England appeared extremely doubtful. Lyman Hall helped persuade him to change his views and he soon became an open advocate of strong and decided action to secure American rights. As a result, he was elected to attend a provincial assembly on January 20, 1776, in Savannah. He was elected by that body to represent Georgia in the Continental Congress. He took his seat in the Congress in May and while he is not known as a major player in the debates, he voted for independence on July 2, for the formal declaration on July 4, and signed his name to the Declaration on August 2.

In October 1776, Gwinnett was again elected to the Georgia assembly and named Speaker and re-elected to the Continental Congress. During his service in the Congress, he was a candidate for a brigadier general position of the 1st Regiment in the Continental Army but lost out to Lachlan McIntosh. Gwinnett was sorely disappointed and embittered and regarded McIntosh as an enemy from that day forward.

In the Georgia Assembly, Gwinnett played an important role in drafting the state's first constitution. When the President (Governor) of Georgia, Archibald Bulloch, died in March 1777, he was appointed to the vacant position by the Assembly's Executive Council. In this position, he was the Commander-In-Chief of Georgia's Militia and he used his power to undermine the leadership of McIntosh. Gwinnett took an active role which caused dissension in the ranks and McIntosh was treated with disrespect by some officers and soldiers. McIntosh had planned an expedition into eastern Florida to secure Georgia's southern border but Governor Gwinnett took over the planning of the expedition and would have led the troops himself but was prevented from doing so due to his position as head of the Provincial Assembly. Instead, he appointed one of McIntosh's subordinates as the commander of the expedition.

The expedition was a failure and Gwinnett and McIntosh publicly blamed each other. Gwinnett was charged with malfeasance but was cleared of all wrongdoing by an inquest. However, he lost his bid for re-election as Governor. On May 1, 1777, Lachlan McIntosh addressed the Georgia assembly denouncing Gwinnett in the harshest terms, calling him "a scoundrel and a lying rascal." Gwinnett called on McIntosh and demanded an apology but McIntosh refused. The consequence was a challenge to a duel sent by Gwinnett and accepted by McIntosh.

They met in the small town of Thunderbolt, near Savannah on May 16, 1777, and fought at a distance of only twelve feet. They were both severely wounded. Gwinnett died of a gangrene infection on May 19 at the age of 45. McIntosh quickly recovered and was charged with murder but acquitted. He went on to live until 1806. Fearing Gwinnett's allies would take revenge on McIntosh, George Washington ordered him to report to Continental Army

The alleged grave of Button Gwinnett at Colonial Park Cemetery in Savannah, Georgia (photo by Joe Farrell).

headquarters in Valley Forge, Pennsylvania, where he spent the winter.

A large beautiful monument in Colonial Park Cemetery marks the site of Gwinnett's grave, though no one is exactly sure it is his. The Colonial Park Cemetery had not been well-maintained into the 1840s and many markers were lost. In 1848, when patriotic citizens wished to move his grave to be with those of Lyman Hall and George Walton beneath the Georgia Signers' Monument in Augusta, Georgia, Gwinnett's remains could not be located. In 1957, retired school principal Arthur Funk began a search for Gwinnett. He located a marker that contained clues linking to Gwinnett and with the help of a New York archaeologist (and permission of the city) began an excavation. Bones were located in the grave that were believed to be Gwinnett's. Controversy raged for several years as the Smithsonian and others weighed in. Some thought the femur had evidence of a musket ball tied to Gwinnett's fatal wounds. Others said the bone was damaged after burial. Some, including the archaeologist, thought the bones were that of a woman. Nonetheless, after much debate, the bones were reinterred in the cemetery and a new monument erected to Gwinnett noting that his bones are "believed to be" here.

Button Gwinnett is memorialized in many places, such as Gwinnett County, Georgia, the Button Gwinnett Elementary School in Hinesville, Georgia, and the Button Gwinnett Chapter of the Sons of the American Revolution in Lawrenceville, Georgia. There is a large monument in Augusta, Georgia to the three Georgia signers of the Declaration of Independence and in 1955 his bust was one of the first three placed in the Georgia Hall of Fame. Gwinnett's signature is considered among the most valuable of historical autographs in the world. This is due to collectors attempting to obtain a complete set of the signers of the Declaration of Independence, as well as his signature being a rarity. Only fifty-one examples of his signature are known to exist. In 1979 a letter signed by Gwinnett brought $100,000 at a New York auction. In 2010 a document bearing his signature sold for $722,000.

Alexander Hamilton

(1755 or 1757–1804)

The Federalist

Buried at Trinity Churchyard,
New York, New York.

U.S. Constitution • Military • Finance • First Secretary of Tresury

When he entered this world, few, if any, would have predicted the legacy left by this Founder. During the Revolution, he served as a trusted aid on the staff of General Washington. He bravely led an attack on British defenses during the decisive Battle of Yorktown. His experience serving in the Continental Army and later in the Continental Congress convinced him that a strong national government was needed if the nation was to survive. He championed that idea during the 1787 Constitutional Convention and was a signer of the document produced by that gathering. He was the principal author of the *Federalist Papers* which proved a vital tool during the ratification process and have endured as a guide to our founding principles. He gained further distinction as the country's first Secretary of the Treasury a role in which he founded the nation's financial system. Born in the West Indies this immigrant became one of the most important and unlikeliest of our Founders. A Broadway musical has reignited interest in his life and contributions. His name, of course, is Alexander Hamilton.

There is a controversy about Hamilton's date of birth. Some historians report that he was born in 1755 while others favor 1757. There is evidence that supports both dates. We do know that Hamilton was born on January 11th to an out-of-wedlock mother in the West Indies. When he was a boy he wrote a vivid account of a hurricane that hit the islands. That work and the abilities he demonstrated working as a clerk impressed a wealthy

Alexander Hamilton portrait by John Trumbull, 1806.

group of men who offered him the chance to study in America. He enrolled at King's College in New York City.

In 1774 when he was just 19, Hamilton addressed a group of patriots who had gathered to hear a number of speakers. His anti-British sentiments impressed those gathered who shouted their support and approval when he concluded his remarks. When an artillery company was organized in the city, Hamilton was chosen as its leader. Later when Washington led his army on a hectic retreat through New Jersey, Hamilton impressed the general with both his wits and skill. Washington made Hamilton one of his top aides. He quickly became one of General Washington's favorites and a father-son relationship developed that, from Washington's view, lasted until his death.

Hamilton distinguished himself throughout the Revolution. He showed his bravery at the decisive Battle of Yorktown when he led a successful assault on British defenses. After the victory,

Hamilton ended his military career and returned to New York to study law. Before the war had ended, in 1780, Hamilton married Elizabeth Schuyler the daughter of Revolutionary War general Phillip Schuyler. The Schuylers were a powerful and wealthy New York family. Despite a later romantic transgression by Hamilton, the marriage was a happy one that produced eight children.

In 1783, Hamilton served as a representative from New York to the Continental Congress. This experience convinced him that the nation could not prosper and might not even survive under the Articles of Confederation. Hamilton wrote to New York's Governor George Clinton saying, "Every day proves more and more the insufficiency of the Confederation. The proselytes to this opinion are fading fast." Hamilton also held the belief that because any act of the Congress required the unanimous consent of the thirteen state legislatures in effect Congress had "no power."

Hamilton was among the delegates representing the state of New York when the Constitutional Convention met in Philadelphia in 1787. He shared the feelings of many of his fellow delegates when he noted that if the assembly failed to establish a stable republican government the result would be that the possibility of such a government succeeding would be "lost to mankind forever." James Madison concurred telling his fellow delegates that they "would decide forever the fate of the republican government." It is not an exaggeration to state that the very survival of the nation depended on the outcome of the convention.

Hamilton favored a strong national government which put him at odds with his fellow delegates from New York as they did not share his views. He actually left the convention on June 29th because of what he viewed as the pigheadedness of his fellow New Yorkers. He returned for a session in August and for the closing ceremony in September. Hamilton signed the Constitution though he disagreed with much of it and viewed it as an initial step to something better.

Despite his reservations, Hamilton threw himself wholeheartedly in the battle to secure the ratification of the Constitution. He authored the majority of the Federalist papers which remain a primary source for divining the intent of the Founders in composing the document. George Washington was impressed by Hamilton and his fellow authors James Madison and John Jay whose work became known as *The Federalist.* Writing to Hamilton, Washington expressed his view that the papers would

Etching of a re-imagined Hamilton and Burr duel.

"merit the notice of posterity because in it are candidly and ably discussed the principles of freedom and the topics of government which will be always interesting to mankind so long as they shall be connected in civil society." The arguments defending the proposed Constitution had a direct impact on the ratification of the Constitution in key states, most notably New York.

On September 11, 1789, Hamilton became the nation's first Secretary of the Treasury. In this position, he shaped the economy of the young nation. His belief in the need for a strong federal government saw him push measures to allow the government to fund the national debt, assume the states' debts, and establish its own bank. Championing these positions often found him at odds with Washington's Secretary of State, Thomas Jefferson, and one of his co-authors of *The Federalist,* James Madison. The disagreements between Hamilton and Jefferson were instrumental in the creation of political parties in the United States.

Hamilton's public service career came to an end as a result of his involvement in the country's first political sex scandal. In 1791, Hamilton began an affair with Maria Lewis Reynolds. When Mr. Reynolds discovered what was going on, he began blackmailing Hamilton by threatening to inform Hamilton's wife. Reynolds was arrested for counterfeiting and hoping for some assistance, he contacted Congressman James Monroe saying he could expose a high government official who was guilty of corruption. Monroe suspected that Reynolds was referring to Hamilton. As part of a Congressional investigation, Monroe and Frederick Muhlenberg interviewed Hamilton who confessed to the affair but denied any misconduct in public office. His explanation was accepted and the parties involved pledged to keep the matter private but in 1797 a newspaper published the details of the affair. Hamilton responded by writing a detailed confession which effectively ended his public service career.

His exit from public service did not include an exit from political affairs. He was active in the 1800 campaign for president. He wrote a pamphlet critical of President John Adams who, like Hamilton, was a member of the Federalist Party. Hamilton, hoping to influence fellow Federalists, sent the document to two hundred members of his party. A Republican postmaster opened a copy and it eventually found its way into the hands of Aaron Burr who was the Republican candidate for vice president. The pamphlet was then printed in Republican papers. The result was that a number of Hamilton's Federalist supporters criticized his actions. One told him that, "some very worthy and sensible men

Grave of Alexander Hamilton at Trinity Church Cemetery in New York City (photo by Joe Farley).

say you have exhibited the same vanity . . . which you charge as a dangerous weakness in Mr. Adams." The episode proved embarrassing for the former Secretary of the Treasury.

In 1804, Hamilton's longtime New York political rival, Vice President Aaron Burr, decided to run for the office of governor in the Empire State. Hamilton fought against Burr who was defeated in the race. Shortly after the election, the *Albany Register* published letters written by Charles Cooper who had attended a dinner party with Hamilton. Cooper noted Hamilton's opposition to Burr and reported that Hamilton had expressed "a still more despicable opinion" of the Vice President at the gathering. Burr saw this as an attack on his honor which set in motion what eventually led to the most famous duel in the history of the United States. On July 11, 1804, Hamilton was mortally wounded in that meeting. He died the following day.

Hamilton was laid to rest in New York's Trinity Churchyard Cemetery. He remains one of the country's most significant Founders. From his service during the Revolution through his championing of the Constitution and service as Secretary of the Treasury, few men played a greater role in the creation of the United States of America.

Elizabeth Schuyler Hamilton
(1757–1854)

The General's Daughter

Buried at Trinity Churchyard Cemetery,
New York, New York.

Thought Leader

She was the second born of the eight children who survived to adulthood produced by the union of Revolutionary War general Philip Schuyler and the wealthy aristocratic Catherine van Rensselaer. For much of her youth and for a time thereafter, she lived in the shadow of her older sister Angelica who was admired for both her looks and her intellect. Both sisters would eventually catch the eye of a young man who served as one of George Washington's aides but it was the younger sister who married Alexander Hamilton becoming Elizabeth Schuyler Hamilton.

Elizabeth, who was often called Betsy, was born on August 9, 1757, in Albany, New York. While her older sister was sent to an exclusive young ladies seminary for her education Betsy received her instructions at home from her mother. As a girl, she was described as something of a tomboy who demonstrated a strong will that she would retain throughout her long and eventful life.

It was in 1780 during the Revolution that Betsy was sent to stay with an aunt in Morristown, New Jersey. It was here she crossed paths with Alexander Hamilton who, along with Washington and his troops, found themselves stationed there during the winter months. The pair had actually met two years prior when Hamilton dined at the Schuyler residence. It was in Morristown that the relationship between Betsy and Hamilton blossomed. That April, with General Schuyler's blessing, they became engaged.

Portrait of the Elizabeth Schuyler Hamilton painted by Ralph Earl while he was in the New York City Jail.

On December 14, 1780, Betsy and Hamilton were married at a gala ceremony staged at the Schuyler Mansion. Since their older daughter, Angelica, had eloped, the General and Mrs. Schuyler spared no expense in celebrating Betsy's wedding. As a matter of fact, General Schuyler urged the couple to take a European honeymoon but Hamilton wouldn't have it. The groom was anxious to get back to the war and he and his new wife went to New Windsor to rejoin Washington's army. It was here that Betsy began aiding Hamilton with his political writings. Portions of Hamilton's 31-page letter to Robert Morris, which illustrates his vast knowledge of finance, are written by her hand. When Betsy became pregnant with the first of their eight children, she returned to her parents' home.

Hamilton continued to press Washington for command of a unit which would see action. Washington eventually granted his request and Hamilton led a successful attack on British defenses during the decisive Battle of Yorktown. After the victory, Hamilton left the army and joined his wife in Albany before the couple settled in New York City in 1783.

In 1789, Hamilton became the nation's first Secretary of the Treasury. While he handled the finances of the country, Betsy did the same for their household. James McHenry remarked to Hamilton that Betsy had "as much merit as your treasurer as you have as Treasurer of the United States." In addition, Betsy continued to aid Hamilton in his political efforts including the work he did on *The Federalist* and his defense of the Bank of the United States.

Betsy was known for her loyalty to her husband in spite of the fact that that loyalty was not always returned. Even when he was courting her back in Morristown, he was having an affair with a local barmaid. Hamilton was attracted to women and women in kind to him and he enjoyed some success in what could be termed woman-handling throughout their marriage. The most notable failure Hamilton experienced in relation to this became known as "The Reynolds Affair."

Though Hamilton had begun his dalliances with Maria Reynolds years earlier, the affair did not become known to the public until 1797, when details appeared in a Republican paper that favored Hamilton's political rival, Thomas Jefferson. Betsy initially didn't believe the reports but Hamilton ended all speculation when he wrote and published a confession that would become known as the *Reynolds Pamphlet*. In it, Hamilton admitted to the affair and to being blackmailed by Maria's husband in order to refute charges that he had been involved in public misconduct with John Reynolds. Through it all, Betsy supported her husband.

In 1797, Betsy's sister Angelica and her husband John Church returned to the United States. The elder sister quickly assumed the leading role in New York and Philadelphia society. Hamilton and Betsy were present at many of the parties hosted by the Churches. Many noted that Hamilton spent much of his time at these soirees dancing with his beautiful sister-in-law. Once again, Betsy ignored the rumors and her legendary loyalty to both her husband and her sister never faltered.

On July 11, 1804, Hamilton was mortally wounded in his historic duel with Vice President Aaron Burr. The next day as he lay dying, he gave Betsy a letter he had written before the duel. In it, he expressed the hope of meeting her in a better world and called her "the best of wives, the best of women."

Betsy would live for fifty years as Hamilton's widow. She spent those years in the service of her husband's memory and greatness. She collected and shared his correspondence, diaries, and political writings including notes to prove that it was her husband who was the primary author of *Washington's Farewell Address.*

Betsy passed away on November 9, 1854, and was laid to rest near her husband in New York's Trinity Churchyard. When she died, she was wearing a locket that contained a yellowed piece of paper. On it was a short poem Hamilton had written for her 74 years before. The poem professed Hamilton's undying affection for the only woman he may have truly loved.

Grave of Elizabeth Schuyler Hamilton at Trinity Church Cemetery in New York City (photo by Lawrence Knorr).

Cornelius Harnett
(1723–1781)
Hero of Cape Fear

Buried at St. James' Churchyard,
Wilmington, North Carolina.

Articles of Confederation

Cornelius Harnett was a wealthy plantation owner and merchant from Wilmington, North Carolina, who was also a Continental Congressman. He was a signer of the Articles of Confederation and died soon after being captured and tortured by the British.

Harnett was born in Edenton, Chowan County, North Carolina, on April 20, 1723. He was the son Cornelius Harnett, Senior, and his wife Elizabeth. The elder Harnett, a native of Ireland, was a colonial official and planter. In 1726, when young Cornelius was three, the family moved to Brunswick Town near what is now Cape Fear, close to the city of Wilmington, North Carolina. In that city, the younger Harnett grew to become a merchant and operated distilleries, businesses, and a schooner in the Cape Fear area. With the proceeds, he purchased a plantation called "Poplar Grove" nearby.

Meanwhile, Brunswick Town had become the busiest port in North Carolina, shipping goods to and from Europe and the British West Indies. When Spanish privateers attacked the first week of September 1748, the townspeople fled to the woods and their homes were looted. A local captain, William Dry, rallied 67 men to expel the invaders. Among them was Cornelius Harnett, Jr. The counterattack was successful. Only one local was killed while ten privateers were killed and thirty captured. One of their two ships exploded, killing most aboard. The second ship was captured and the goods and slaves recovered. The contraband that

Etching of "Poplar Grove," the home of Cornelius Harnett near Wilmington, North Carolina.

was captured was subsequently sold to fund St. Philip's Church in Brunswick Town and St. James' Church in Wilmington.

In 1750, Harnett was elected as a member of the Wilmington city commission and appointed as a justice of the peace, where he served until 1777. In 1754, Harnett was elected to a seat in the North Carolina General Assembly. He took a leading role in that body following the passage of the Stamp Act by the British Parliament. Harnett joined in the march in Brunswick Town in February 1766 to openly protest the act. He became a leading voice against the royal governor, William Tryon, and became chairman of the local Sons of Liberty. In June 1770, Harnett led the resistance to the Townshend Acts, effectively boycotting British imports.

In December 1773, following the Boston Tea Party, Harnett joined the first Committee of Correspondence in North Carolina. He subsequently joined the North Carolina Council of Safety in 1776 as war with Britain was underway. Harnett was unanimously elected the group's president, becoming North Carolina's first (unelected) chief executive as an independent state. In this role, Harnett corresponded with political and military leaders. He also personally took up arms against the British, marching with General John Ashe to sack the British encampment at Fort

Johnson. This drew the attention of the British who put a bounty on his head.

In 1776, Harnett served in the North Carolina provincial congresses in Halifax, North Carolina, and was chairman of the committee that drafted the state constitution. Under his direction, the group sent a document to the Continental Congress, now known as the "Halifax Resolves," calling for a declaration of independence from England. This was the first official action by a colony that called for separation from England.

Harnett was elected to the Continental Congress in May of 1777, just in time for Congress to abandon Philadelphia after the British occupation. Later that year, Harnett participated in the formulation of the Articles of Confederation to which he was a signer. Harnett returned to North Carolina at great risk at a time when the British were reasserting control throughout the south.

In January 1781, the British took Wilmington, North Carolina. Harnett, who was suffering from gout, was recuperating at a friend's house thirty miles away. He was found and captured by British Major James Craig's marauders. His hands and feet were tied and he was tossed across a horse "like a sack of meal." Harnett was carried back to town where he was thrown in a blockhouse that had no roof. Exposed to the elements, Cornelius succumbed on April 18, 1781.

Grave of Cornelius Harnett at St. James Churchyard Cemetery in Wilmington, North Carolina (photo by Lawrence Knorr).

Harnett was laid to rest in St. James' Churchyard in Wilmington, North Carolina. He has a nondescript stone stating an incorrect date of death. Harnett County, North Carolina, is named in his honor. Harnett had married Mary Holt, but the couple had no children. She died in 1792.

John Hart
(1713–1779)

Washington Camped Here

Buried at Hopewell Baptist Meeting House Cemetery,
Hopewell, New Jersey.

Declaration of Independence

John Hart was a public official in colonial New Jersey who, although he received very little formal schooling, developed a reputation for honesty and generosity that led him to be selected as a delegate to the Second Continental Congress and a signer of the Declaration of Independence.

Sources disagree as to the year and place of Hart's birth but most biographers have put it in 1713, in Hopewell, New Jersey. He was named for his grandfather who was a carpenter from Long Island. John's father Edward was a farmer, Justice of the Peace, and leader of a local militia unit during the French and Indian War. Edward moved to Hopewell at about the age of 20, married Martha Furman in 1712, and they had five children.

John was baptized at the Maidenhead Meetinghouse (now the Presbyterian Church of Lawrenceville) on December 31, 1713. He learned to read and write and do math but received very little formal education. He was a poor speller but was well known for his common sense and considered knowledgeable about money and business matters. He was attracted to a young lady named Deborah Scudder and rode thirty miles round trip to see her. They married in 1739 and had 13 children. In 1740, he started to acquire land and soon was the largest landowner in Hopewell. In 1747, he donated a piece of his land to local Baptists who had been seeking a place to build a church. John was a Presbyterian and thus his donation endeared him to the Baptists in the area.

Portrait of John Hart, artist unknown.

John Hart began his public service in 1750 when he was elected to the Hunterdon County Board of Chosen Freeholders, the highest elected office in the county. In 1755, he was elected Justice of the Peace and was thereafter called John Hart, Esquire.

In 1761, he was elected to the Provincial Assembly of New Jersey. There he pressed for New Jersey to participate in the Stamp Act Congress, in New York in 1765. He was particularly disgusted with the Stamp Act. The tax was trifling but it involved a principle. It gave the Crown power over the colonies against the arbitrary exercise of which they had no protection. This meant that they had little control over their own property. It might be taxed in the manner and to the extent which Parliament pleased, and not a single voice represented the colonies.

He would serve in that assembly until 1771. In 1768, he was appointed as a judge to the Court of Common Pleas. He was often called "Honest John." In 1775, he was elected to the Committee of Correspondence of New Jersey which was a vehicle for the colonies to keep each other informed about developments regarding the Revolution.

In 1776, New Jersey formed a revolutionary assembly and Hart was elected and served as vice president. The New Jersey delegation to the First Continental Congress was opposed to independence. On June 22, 1776, he was elected as one of five New Jersey delegates to the Second Continental Congress with authorization to vote for independence. His fellow delegates were Abraham Clark, Francis Hopkinson, Richard Stockton, and John Witherspoon. Hart voted for the Declaration of Independence and was the thirteenth to sign it. He and the others were now branded traitors by King George III.

The fine grave of John Hart at Hopewell Baptist Meeting House Cemetery in Hopewell, New Jersey (photo by Lawrence Knorr).

He served in Congress until August and then was elected to the New Jersey State Assembly where days later he was elected its speaker. On October 5, he returned home to attend to his sick wife. On October 8, 1776, Deborah Hart died.

On November 13, the British invaded the state and in December advanced into Hunterdon County. A marked man due to his status as Speaker of the Assembly, Hart had to hide from the British and the Hessians who were hunting for him, at one point hiding in a natural rock formation called the Rock House. The Hessians ravaged the Hopewell area and Hart's home and property suffered severe damage. Two of his young children took refuge in the homes of relatives. Great effort was made to capture him and fellow New Jersey signer Richard Stockton. Though Hart was able to elude the British, Stockton was not and was held under deplorable conditions. The Continentals capture of Trenton on December 26 allowed Hart to return home. He collected his

Detail from John Hart's monument (photo by Lawrence Knorr).

family and went to work repairing his home and farm. He was re-elected twice as Speaker of the Assembly and served until November 1778.

In June 1778, Hart invited the American army to camp at his farm. Washington accepted his invitation and 12,000 men occupied his fields from June 22 to June 24 and at least once General Washington dined with their host. Two days after leaving, the troops fought the British at the Battle of Monmouth.

On November 7, 1778, Hart returned from the Assembly in Trenton. Two days later, he was too sick with "gravel" (kidney stones) to return. He continued to suffer a slow and painful death until he succumbed on May 11, 1779, at the age of 66.

John Hart and his wife were laid to rest at the Hopewell Baptist Meeting House Cemetery on the same ground that Hart had donated for the building of the Baptist church. His grave is marked by a beautiful obelisk and bronze plaque. The date on the obelisk for his death is 1780 but most biographers and the *New Jersey Gazette* say he died on May 11, 1779.

Next to Hart's grave is the grave of Joab Houghton. A memorial to him was erected by the people of Hopewell and dedicated in 1896. On the face of the memorial is inscribed "Sunday, April 23, 1775, news of the Battle of Lexington reached

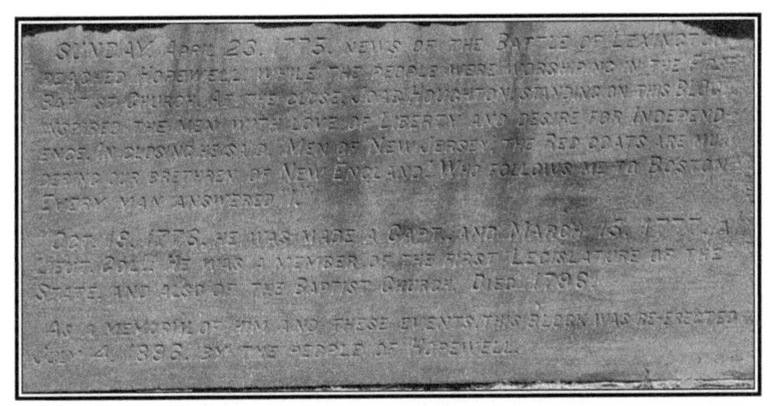

Detail of the monument honoring Joab Houghton at Hopewell Baptist Meeting House Cemetery (photo by Lawrence Knorr).

Hopewell when the people were worshiping in the First Baptist Church. At the close, Joab Houghton, standing on this stone, inspired the men with love of liberty and desire for independence. In closing, he said, "Men of New Jersey, the Red Coats are murdering your brethren in New England! Who follows me to Boston?" Every man said "Aye". Houghton went on to serve as a lieutenant colonel in the Revolutionary Army.

Joseph Hewes
(1730–1779)

First Secretary of Naval Affairs

Buried at Christ Church Burial Ground,
Philadelphia, Pennsylvania.

Continental Association • Declaration of Independence

This Founder was born in New Jersey but made his mark representing the state of North Carolina. He was raised by his Quaker parents. He attended Princeton College. He then decided to go into business and moved to Philadelphia to serve as an apprentice to the successful merchant and importer Joseph Ogden. He learned enough to become a very successful merchant on his own. Already an established businessman by the age of thirty, he relocated to North Carolina. It was in his adopted state that he made a name for himself politically when he was elected to the first Continental Congress in 1774. He was still in Congress when that body declared American independence and he proudly signed the document authored by Thomas Jefferson. He is also credited with playing a leading role in the creation of the Continental Navy and many consider him the first Secretary of the Navy. His name was Joseph Hewes.

Hewes was born on January 23, 1730, in Kingston, New Jersey. There is no dispute as to the fact that he attended Princeton College. What is in dispute is whether or not he graduated. Diploma or not, he was determined to make his way in the world of business. He worked initially as an apprentice in Philadelphia before establishing his own successful business. In1760 at the age of thirty, he moved to Edenton, North Carolina which was a growing seaport on the Albemarle Sound. He successfully built a thriving business there as well but, while his

Etching of a portrait of Joseph Hewes, artist unknown.

professional life produced prosperity, his personal life produced heartbreak. Hewes was engaged to be married to the love of his life, Isabella Johnston, who died just days before their planned wedding. He would never marry.

Hewes was active in North Carolina's political affairs and was elected to the state legislature just three years after he settled there. Though he was an advocate for the rights of the colonies, he did not hold the view that separation from the mother country was best for America. It was a position he would champion up to the day Congress passed the motion declaring America's independence.

In 1774, North Carolina elected Hewes to the First Continental Congress. As a member of Congress, he supported measures that would harm his business interests. He strongly supported and worked to establish a nonimportation association. Since much of his own business dealings involved British imports, this action cost him dearly from a financial standpoint. But money was not all this patriot sacrificed for his country.

In 1775, the Quakers held a convention which denounced the Congress of which Hewes was a member. They announced that they opposed both war and the committees of Congress formed to aid in the American effort. Hewes responded by ending his affiliation with the Quakers siding with his nation against the religious beliefs of his parents.

Hewes was noted for being a hard and tireless worker in Congress. It appears that he applied the same energy, resolve, and determination he had used to build his business in his role as a representative of his state. Absenteeism was a major problem in Congress. By the fall of 1775, often more than 30% of the delegates were missing when the delegates were called to order. Hewes seldom missed even a committee meeting. In the momentous month of July 1776, he described his work as "too severe" noting that he sometimes attended meetings for eleven to twelve hours at a stretch "without eating or drinking." His health suffered but he refused to lessen his workload writing that he "obstinately persisted in doing my duty to the best of my judgment and abilities, and attended Congress the whole time, one day excepted."

Grave of Joseph Hewes at Christ Church Burial Ground in Philadelphia, Pennsylvania (photo by Joe Farley).

As the mood in Congress shifted toward declaring independence, Hewes remained convinced that the colonies could achieve their objectives without separating from England. Though he still hoped for reconciliation with the mother country, he put his ships at the nation's disposal. He also used his influence to push hard to get a navy commander's assignment for a friend of his by the name of John Paul Jones. Hewes worked on a committee to rig the first navy ship and served as Secretary of the Naval Affairs Committee. Though he is in competition for the title with his friend Jones, many believe that it is Hewes who deserves to be called the "Father of the Navy."

When Richard Henry Lee introduced his resolution to declare independence in June of 1776, Hewes still felt that the action was premature. It was through the efforts of John Adams that Hewes was finally convinced to vote for independence. Adams would later recall "the unanimity of the States finally depended upon the vote of Joseph Hewes, and was finally determined by him." As for Hewes himself, after the resolution was adopted he lifted both hands and called out, "It is done! And I will abide by it."

In 1779, Hewes was still hard at work in Congress. He grew ill, probably as a result of overwork and undernourishment. Keeping his shoulder to the plow, he wrote, "My country is entitled to my services, and I shall not shrink from her cause, even though it should cost me my life." It did. Too ill to travel home to North Carolina, he died on October 10, 1779, at the age of 49. He was laid to rest in the Christ Church Burial Ground and his fellow congressmen wore a black crape around their arms for a month in his memory.

In 1894, an effort was made to move Hewes' remains back to North Carolina. On May 24th of that year, the *Wilmington Messenger* reported that his grave was lost. The paper noted that Hewes had been buried in the cemetery of Christ Episcopal Church in Philadelphia but that a "patient search failed to find either the grave or any record of it on the archives of the church." In 2003, the Christ Church Preservation Society published a small book written by Jean K. Wolf titled *Lives of the Silent Stones in the Christ Church Burial Ground.* In it, the author explains that the cemetery contains a donated commemorative plaque honoring Hewes because "the 1864 inscription book lists no grave marker for Joseph Hewes." Thus the burial site of this patriot and significant Founder is unmarked.

Jared Ingersoll
(1749 – 1822)

Pennsylvania Attorney General

Buried at Old Pine Street Presbyterian Church Cemetery,
Philadelphia, Pennsylvania.

U.S. Constitution

This Founder's father was a British colonial official and later a loyalist during the American Revolution. Though he initially shared his father's views, he would evolve and fully commit to the cause of American independence. He studied the law and became a leading Philadelphia attorney. He was elected to and served in the Continental Congress in 1780-81. In 1787, he was one of the delegates representing Pennsylvania at the Constitutional Convention and he signed the document that was created by that gathering. He would later serve as the Attorney General of Pennsylvania, the United States District Attorney for Pennsylvania, and the presiding judge of the Philadelphia District Court. In 1812, he was the Federalist candidate for the office of Vice President. His name was Jared Ingersoll.

Ingersoll was born on November 7, 1749, in New Haven Connecticut. He received a solid education and graduated from Yale in 1766. He then studied law in Philadelphia and was admitted to the Pennsylvania bar in 1773. His father was a British colonial agent who had actually served in the position of Stamp Master in Connecticut after the Stamp Act was imposed on the colonies in 1765. After assuming that position, the elder Ingersoll became one of the most hated men in his colony. The Sons of Liberty hung his effigy on August 21 of the same year he took that office.

In 1773, with revolutionary passions running high, Ingersoll, heeding his father's advice, sailed to London to continue his study

Portrait of Jared Ingersoll etched by Albert Rosenthal, 1888, based on a painting by Charles Willson Peale.

of law and travel throughout Europe. During this time, he spent 18 months in Paris where he was welcomed by Benjamin Franklin who was a friend of the family. One of the reasons he left England for France was the news that the colonies had declared their independence. Shortly after the colonies' declaration, Ingersoll broke with his family's views and made a personal commitment to the patriot cause. He didn't view remaining in England as an option. He returned to America in 1778, arriving in Philadelphia where, with the help of friends, not the least being Joseph Reed the president of the state, he established a successful law practice.

In 1780-81 he was elected to and served in the Continental Congress. After the Revolution, Ingersoll became convinced that the Articles of Confederation had to be amended if the union was to survive. He was chosen as one of Pennsylvania's representatives to the 1787 Constitutional Convention. He entered the convention

Grave of Jared Ingersoll at Old Pine Street Presbyterian Church Cemetery, Philadelphia, Pennsylvania (photo by Joe Farley).

believing that the Articles merely needed to be amended to render them effective. He was a regular though silent representative at the gathering in Philadelphia. He spoke but once at the convention and left behind no written recollections of the assembly except his signature on the Constitution itself. He did later say that he did not believe his signing of the document should be regarded as a pledge to support it in every particular describing it as "a recommendation of what, all things considered, was the most eligible." He would get the opportunity to argue several cases before the United States Supreme Court that aided in ironing out some of the finer points regarding constitutional law.

After the Constitution was ratified, Ingersoll devoted his energies to service to the city of Philadelphia as a judge and to his state as the Attorney General. He remained a Federalist who ardently

Detail from Jared Ingersoll's gravestone (photo by Joe Farley).

opposed the election of Thomas Jefferson in 1800. In 1812, he became the candidate for Vice President on the Federalist ticket headed by DeWitt Clinton. The Federalists failed in their attempt to defeat President James Madison, losing the electoral vote by a 128 to 89 margin. Ingersoll failed to deliver the crucial electoral votes of his home state.

Also at Old Pine Street Presbyterian Church Cemetery is the grave of William Hurry who was tasked with ringing the Liberty Bell to announce the passing of the Declaration of Independence on July 4, 1776 (photo by Joe Farley).

Ingersoll passed away at the age of 72, just a week before his 73rd birthday, on October 31, 1822, in Philadelphia. He was laid to rest in the Old Pine Street Presbyterian Church Cemetery located in that city. It was said of Ingersoll that he had one conviction that stood out, it being that patriots should serve for the honor of one thing, for the glory of their country, and never just as a means of livelihood or selfish prestige.

Daniel of St. Thomas Jenifer
(1723–1790)
Elder Statesman

Probably buried at "Ellerslie" plantation family plot,
Port Tobacco, Maryland.

U.S. Constitution

Daniel of St. Thomas Jenifer was a plantation owner and Maryland politician who participated in the Continental Congress and signed the United States Constitution.

He was the son of Dr. Daniel Jenifer and Elizabeth Mason of Charles County, Maryland, near the town of Port Tobacco. The Jenifers' estate was then known as "Coates Retirement" (or "Retreat") and later "Ellerslie." The elder Jenifer was of English and Swedish ancestry. The reason for the linkage to St. Thomas is unclear. Some have surmised there was a family connection to either St. Thomas in the Virgin Islands or to the Parish of St. Thomas in County Cornwall, England.

Daniel was a popular name in the Jenifer family. The Founding Father's great-grandfather was Captain Daniel Jenifer (1637-1692/3) of Accomack County, Virginia, who later moved to Maryland. His son was Daniel of St. Thomas Jenifer (1672–1730). Then came Dr. Daniel (1699-1729) who had two sons, the Founder with the St. Thomas middle name, and another named (just) Daniel (1727-1795). That Daniel, the brother of the Founder, had two sons; one named Daniel of St. Thomas Jenifer who died unmarried and one named Dr. Daniel Jenifer (1756-1809). This nephew subsequently had sons named Daniel of St. Thomas Jenifer (1789-1822) and Colonel Daniel Jenifer (1791-1855), who was a congressman and ambassador. This Daniel carried on the tradition of two sons; one named Daniel and another named

Oil on canvas portrait of Daniel of St. Thomas Jenifer by John Hesselius.

Daniel of St. Thomas (1814-1843). Daniel of St. Thomas Jenifer, the Founder, was also the uncle of fellow Founder Thomas Stone as well as Michael Jenifer Stone and John Hoskins Stone.

Little is known about Daniel's childhood and education. Into young adulthood, he lived on and managed the estate near Port Tobacco before moving to Annapolis. Later in life, he lived at a plantation called "Stepney" near Annapolis. Throughout his life, Jenifer was a substantial landowner and traded in slaves and indentured servants. He also had stakes in several local industries.

During the colonial period, prior to the Revolution, Jenifer acted as receiver-general for absentee proprietors in Maryland, collecting taxes and rents. He was well-liked and trusted by the locals, rising to justice of the peace and serving in many capacities including as a trusted advisor of the last royal governor of Maryland, Sir Robert Eden.

In 1760, Jenifer served on a boundary commission that helped settle the border disputes between Maryland, Pennsylvania, Delaware, and Virginia. Two English surveyors, Mason and Dixon, were hired from England to survey the boundaries.

As tensions mounted between the colonies and England, Jenifer put his economic might behind the patriot cause. He became the president of Maryland's Council of Safety that helped establish and organize the state militia. Later, he was president of the first state senate (1777-80), sat in the Continental Congress (1778-82), and held the position of Maryland state revenue and financial manager (1782-85). In his roles, Jenifer mostly served as a land manager, tracking and disposing of loyalist properties seized by patriots. He also used his deft financial management skills to help the state survive the postwar economic depression. Along with his friends George Washington, James Madison, George Mason, and John Dickinson, Jenifer worked collectively on solving the new nation's financial issues. To that end, he attended the Mount Vernon Conference, a precursor to the Constitutional Convention.

Jenifer was not the first choice to represent Maryland at the Constitutional Convention in Philadelphia, but when one of the

"Ellerslie" near Port Tobacco where the body of Daniel of St. Thomas Jenifer is buried somewhere on the grounds.

four candidates backed out, he was asked to fill in. Upon his arrival, Jenifer was one of the elder statesmen present, younger only than his good friend Benjamin Franklin and Roger Sherman.

Despite his advancing years and physical limitations, Jenifer was one of only 29 delegates (of 55) who attended nearly every session. While he did not speak much, he used his good nature and humor to influence his colleagues and encourage compromise.

Philosophically, despite representing a small state, Jenifer was for Madison's Virginia Plan which espoused a strong central government with taxing authority. This put him at odds with fellow Marylander Luther Martin and given the regular absence of the two other delegates from the state, left them deadlocked. However, regarding the composition of the Senate, Martin was for equal representation among the states, as were the other smaller states. Out of courtesy, though he disagreed, the elderly Jenifer ambled out of Carpenter's Hall that July afternoon to allow Martin to vote on behalf of Maryland. He then returned to sign the Constitution, though Martin did not affix his signature.

Said Martin, "If the people support the Constitution, I will be hanged."

Jenifer quipped, "You should stay in Philadelphia so they don't get you with their ropes!"

After the convention, Jenifer returned to "Stepney" and lived out his remaining years, passing away in 1790. Daniel never married. He left most of his massive 10,000+ acre estate to his nephew Daniel Jenifer. He requested his slaves be freed six years after his death. He also bequeathed all his French-language books in his library to his good friend James Madison.

The exact location of Daniel of St. Thomas Jenifer's grave is unknown. Some suggest he was buried at "Stepney," while most believe he is buried in an unmarked grave at "Ellerslie" near Port Tobacco.

Jenifer Streets in Madison, Wisconsin and Washington, D.C. are named in his honor.

Francis Lightfoot Lee
(1734–1797)
Virginia Congressman

Buried at Tayloe Family Burial Ground,
Warsaw, Virginia.

Declaration of Independence • Articles of Confederation

Francis Lightfoot Lee, the brother of Richard Henry Lee and cousin of "Light Horse Harry" Lee, was a Continental Congressman who signed the Declaration of Independence and Articles of Confederation. He was also a member of the Virginia state House of Delegates and the state Senate.

Lee was born October 14, 1734, at "Machadoc," later known as "Burnt House Field," in Hague, Westmoreland County, Virginia. After the completion of "Stratford Hall," in Westmoreland County, Virginia, a few years later, the family moved there. He was the fourth son, and one of eleven children, of Thomas Lee, a planter in Virginia, and his wife Hannah Harrison (née Ludwell) Lee. Thomas Lee was a leading Virginia planter with over 30,000 acres of land prior to his death in 1750.

Francis was taught by private tutors at "Stratford Hall." When his parents died in 1750, the estate was left to the older children, leaving out Francis and his younger siblings. His oldest brother, Phillip Lee, controlled his parents' assets. Francis and the younger children sued in court for a portion but lost. Eventually, Francis reconciled with his brother and was granted one of the family estates in Loudon County.

Lee then got into politics and ran for a seat in the Virginia House of Burgesses in which he served from 1758 to 1768. Lee's first patriotic action was his protest of The Stamp Act. He signed

Portrait of Francis Lightfoot Lee, artist unknown.

the Westmoreland Resolves which was a business protest of the act that played a part in the repeal of The Stamp Act.

In 1769, Lee married his second cousin Rebecca Plater Tayloe and moved from Loudon to Richmond County where his father-in-law had gifted them "Menokin" plantation on which to reside. He was again elected to the House of Burgesses but only served occasionally. From 1770 to 1774, he was a justice of the peace for his new Richmond County. He also served in that position for Loudon County in 1771.

In March 1775, a convention of delegates gathered in Richmond to organize for the Revolution. Lee was one of the delegates from Richmond. In August of that year, Lee was appointed to the Continental Congress and moved to Philadelphia with his wife, staying with his sister and brother-in-law, William Shippen, who himself was later a Continental Congressman. Lee served in

"Mount Airy" Plantation where Francis Lightfoot Lee is buried (photo by Lawrence Knorr).

the Continental Congress into 1779, but biographers recorded that he rarely spoke, though his opinions were valued.

The Reverend Charles Goodrich wrote in 1842,

> During his attendance upon this body, he seldom took part in the public discussions, but few surpassed him in his warmth of patriotism, and in his zeal to urge forward those measures which contributed to the success of the American arms, and the independence of the country. To his brother, Richard Henry Lee, the high honor was allotted of bringing forward the momentous question of independence, and to him, and his associates in that distinguished assembly, the not inferior honor was granted of aiding and supporting and finishing this important work.

Robert T. Conrad added in 1846, "Although not gifted with the powers of oratory, his good sense, extensive reading, and sound and discriminating judgment, made him a useful member of the house."

It is believed Francis Lee signed the Declaration of Independence with many others in August 1776. In an 1821 letter to painter John Trumbull in a Washington newspaper, the artist was critiqued for not including Francis Lee in the painting of the signers, though many who were not present on July 4 were included in it.

Lee continued in the Congress until he resigned in April of 1779, having also signed the Articles of Confederation before they were ratified. He returned to Virginia and served in the state senate for a period, but then retired. In 1788, he clashed with his brother, Richard Henry Lee, when he supported ratification of the Constitution.

Francis Lee died of pleurisy at "Menokin" on January 11, 1797, at the age of 62, only four days after his wife passed. *The American Minerva* newspaper of New York City printed an obituary,

> Died. At his seat in Richmond County, on Wednesday, the 18th ultimo, in the sixty-third year of his age, Francis Lightfoot Lee, Esquire. He was an early, zealous and active friend to the revolution, which established the independence of the United States of America. He was a firm, calm, and enlightened patriot, and a most unequaled social companion.

Lee and his wife were laid to rest at the Tayloe's "Mount Airy" plantation near Warsaw, Virginia. The authors were unable to visit the graves which are on private property posted with a sign threatening gunshots if dust was seen in the driveway.

In 1877, Mark Twain wrote about Lee,

> This man's life-work was so inconspicuous, that his name would now be wholly forgotten, but for one thing—he signed the Declaration of Independence. Yet his life was a most useful and worthy one. It was a good and profitable voyage, though it left no phosphorescent splendors in its wake.

Francis and Rebecca Lee had no children; his namesake Francis Lightfoot Lee II was the son of his brother Richard Henry Lee, and further men of the same name descend from him.

Henry Lee III
(1756–1818)

Lighthorse Harry

Buried at Lee Chapel at Washington and Lee University,
Lexington, Virginia.

Military

Henry Lee III, known as "Light-Horse Harry" Lee, was a cavalry officer during the American Revolution. He served in the Continental Congress (1785-88) where he pushed for the reform of the Articles of Confederation. He then served as governor of Virginia and in the U.S. House of Representatives where he is remembered for his eulogy of the late George Washington. He was the father of Robert E. Lee, the Confederate commander in the Civil War.

Henry Lee III was born on January 29, 1756, at "Leesylvania," the family estate near Dumfries, Prince William County, Virginia. He was the son of Henry Giles Lee II and Lucy (née Grymes) Lee. His brother, Charles Lee (1758-1815) served as Attorney General under President George Washington (1795-97). These Lees were cousins to the Lees of "Stratford Hall" which included Richard Henry Lee and Francis Lightfoot Lee.

Young Henry was tutored at home and then entered the College of New Jersey (now Princeton), graduating in 1773 at the age of 17. He was prepared to go to England to study law, but the onset of the American Revolution prevented it. Instead, he received military training and was commissioned as a captain in the Virginia Dragoons on June 18, 1776.

An excellent horseman, Lee was quickly promoted and soon found himself in charge of three troops of cavalry and three companies of infantry dubbed Lee's Legion. At Paulus Hook, near New York harbor, he surprised the enemy post and captured 160 men,

Portrait of Henry "Lighthorse Harry" Lee, III, by William Edward West.

bayonets, and ammunition earning the nickname "Light-Horse Harry" and resulting in the gift of a gold medal from Congress—the only such medal given to someone of lower rank than general. This meteoric rise as a young officer led to him being arrogant and intolerant of criticism. He was twice before boards of court-martial.

Now a lieutenant colonel, in 1780 Lee was assigned to the Southern Department under Nathanael Greene. Lee's Legion raided the British outpost of Georgetown, South Carolina with General Francis Marion in January 1781. He acted as the rear guard of the American army, harassing the British as Greene's troops continued a strategic retreat through the Carolinas to cross the Dan River into Virginia in February. He then combined with Francis Marion and Andrew Pickens to capture numerous British outposts in South Carolina and Georgia. Along the way, they terrorized Loyalists throughout the region highlighted by Pyle's Massacre on February 24, 1781. At Guilford Courthouse

(March 15, 1781), Lee's troops fought to a draw, but Lee failed to communicate with Greene, leading to a collapse of the lines and an American retreat. Lee then saw action at Eutaw Springs in September 1781. Lee stayed in the service of Greene during the remainder of the successful Southern Campaign and was present at Yorktown for Cornwallis's surrender there.

With the British defeated, Lee resigned his commission and returned to Virginia. There he married his cousin, Matilda Ludwell Lee, known as "Divine Matilda," in 1782. The couple had three children who lived past infancy: Philip Ludwell Lee (1784–1794), Lucy Grymes Lee (1786–1860), and Henry Lee IV (1787–1837). The latter was a historian and author who served as a speechwriter for both John C. Calhoun and presidential candidate Andrew Jackson. He helped to write Jackson's inaugural address.

Now a private citizen, and close friend of George Washington, Lee entered politics and was elected to the Virginia House of Delegates in 1785. On November 15, that body selected him to a seat in the Continental Congress. He attended sessions through 1788, writing that the government was in shambles without proper financing or foreign policy. Wrote historian Thomas Templin in his biography of Lee:

> Lee was, of course, well aware of the condition of the national government before he went to New York to sit in Congress. Even so, he seems to have been shaken by the impotency which he found there. His arrival came at a somewhat inauspicious time: Congress was virtually crippled by the non-attendance of sufficient members to conduct business, and it was engaged in a frustrating discussion of how to deal with the unwillingness of Georgia and New York to consent to a revised impost measure. On 16 February [1785] Lee wrote Washington and Madison on "the dreadful situation of our federal government," referring to the inertia of Congress, the dreary outlook for obtaining money needed to meet obligations, and the poor diplomatic position of the United States with respect to Britain, the Barbary States, and the western Indians. Lee's appraisal of the government was "its death cannot be very far distant unless immediate and adequate exertions are made by the several states."

Lee pushed for the reform of the Articles of Confederation, which was replaced by the U.S. Constitution. Lee was a delegate to the Virginia convention that ratified the Constitution in 1788.

Lee was greatly affected by the death of his wife in 1790. He grieved and focused on family for nearly two years. Then, he was elected Governor of Virginia in 1792, serving for three years. In 1793, he married Anne Hill Carter with whom they had six children: Algernon Sidney Lee (1795–1796), Charles Carter Lee (1798–1871), Anne Kinloch Lee (1800–1864), Sydney Smith Lee (1802–1869), Robert Edward Lee (1807–1870), and Mildred Lee (1811–1856).

In 1794, President Washington asked Lee to command the nearly 13,000 federal troops to put down the Whiskey Rebellion in western Pennsylvania. Washington had ridden at the head of the column through Pennsylvania along with Lee. He then handed the army to Alexander Hamilton after they joined up at Fort Cumberland. This rebellion was put down without a loss of life.

In 1798, Lee was appointed Major General, in anticipation of war of France. Later that year, he was elected to the Sixth Congress (1799-1801), where he was best known for the eulogy of the late President Washington, calling him "first in war, first in peace, and first in the hearts of his countrymen."

After leaving Congress, Lee retired to the family estate, "Stratford Hall," in Virginia, but struggled financially due to the Panic of 1796-97 and the bankruptcy of Robert Morris. In 1808, in anticipation of war with Britain, Lee was again commissioned a major general by Thomas Jefferson and he began organizing the Virginia militia. The following year, Lee became bankrupt and

Lee Chapel at Washington and Lee University in Lexington, Virginia (photo by Lawrence Knorr).

served one year in debtors' prison in Montross, Virginia, after which he moved the family to Alexandria, Virginia.

As the War of 1812 was about to break out, Lee appealed to President Madison to serve again in the military, but Madison refused. Around this time, he published his *Memoirs of the War in the Southern Department of the United States* where he recounted his military experiences during the Revolutionary War. During the civil unrest in Baltimore, Maryland in July of 1812, Lee was severely beaten and left for dead on the street. As a Federalist, he and others had opposed the War of 1812 and were present to defend newspaperman and friend Alexander Handon. The group was jailed by Baltimore city officials. A mob led by George Woolslager then broke into the jail, removed the Federalists, and beat and tortured them. One, James Lingan, died.

Lee was greatly affected by his injuries to his body, head, and face, and suffered a speech impediment. He went to the West Indies in 1817, and while returning the following year, stopped to convalesce at his old commander Nathanael Greene's daughter's home near St. Mary's, Georgia. He died there on March 25, 1818, at the age of 62. His body was initially buried in a crypt near the home in Dungeness, Georgia, with full military honors.

In 1862, as Robert E. Lee was reviewing military defenses near Cumberland Island, Georgia, he visited the grave of his father, a man he barely knew. In May 1913, Lee's remains were exhumed and buried next to Robert E. Lee's under the Lee Chapel at Washington and Lee University in Lexington, Virginia.

Crypt of Henry Lee, III, beneath the Lee Chapel, next to his son Robert E. Lee (photo by Lawrence Knorr).

Richard Henry Lee
(1732–1794)

Resolution for Independence

Buried at Lee Family Plot,
"Burnt House Field" plantation, Coles Point, Virginia.

Continental Association • Declaration of Independence
Articles of Confederation • President of Congress

Richard Henry Lee, the brother of Francis Lightfoot Lee and cousin of "Light Horse Harry" Lee, was a Continental Congressman who signed the Continental Association, Declaration of Independence, and Articles of Confederation. He was also the President of Congress (1784-1785). He is best known for proposing the Lee Resolution, the motion in the Continental Congress calling for independence from Great Britain. He was also a United States Senator from (1789-1792).

Lee was born January 26, 1732, at "Machadoc," later known as "Burnt House Field," in Hague, Westmoreland County, Virginia. He was the fifth son, and one of eleven children, of Thomas Lee, a planter in Virginia, and his wife Hannah Harrison (née Ludwell) Lee. Thomas Lee, the president of the Virginia Colonial Council, was a leading Virginia planter with over 30,000 acres of land prior to his death in 1750. After the completion of "Stratford Hall," in Westmoreland County, Virginia, a few years later, the family moved there.

Richard was taught by private tutors at "Stratford Hall." He was then sent to England to study at Wakefield Academy in Yorkshire. When his parents died in 1750, his oldest brother, Phillip Lee, urged him to return home, but he refused, instead going on a tour of mainland Europe.

Portrait of Richard Henry Lee by Charles Willson Peale.

Richard returned to the colonies in 1753 and continued his studies. In 1755, during the French and Indian War, he was named the head of a volunteer militia serving under General Edward Braddock. Fortunately for Lee, Braddock did not utilize his unit and he saw no action nor did he play a role in the fateful Braddock Expedition. Lee married Anne Aylett in December 1757, and settled at his plantation, "Chantilly-on-the Potomac," near "Stratford Hall." Richard and Anne had four children—two sons and two daughters. The following year, while hunting, Lee's gun exploded in his hands, taking all but one finger on his left hand. For the remainder of his life, Lee wore a glove to cover up the wound. Later that same year, Anne Lee died of pleurisy.

In 1764, Lee was named to a committee by the House of Burgesses to send a message to the king calling for an end to harmful economic measures being enacted against the colonies. In February 1766, Lee was one of the leading figures behind the establishment of the Westmoreland Association. One surviving draft of that document in Lee's hand stated,

> . . . the Birthright privilege of every British subject (and of the people of Virginia as being such) founded on Reason, Law, and Compact; that he cannot be legally tried but by his peers; and that he cannot be taxed, but by the consent of a Parliament, in which he is represented by persons chosen by the people. The Stamp Act does absolutely direct the property of the people to be taken from them without their consent.

In 1767, Lee was a justice of the peace in Westmoreland County. The following year, he was elected to the Virginia House of Burgesses, taking the seat of his brother Philip. He served until 1775 along with his brothers Thomas Ludwell Lee and Francis Lightfoot Lee. In this body, he railed against slavery wanting to tax it into oblivion. He believed slaves were entitled to equal freedom and liberty. Such views put him at odds with most of the men in that body. In 1769, Lee married Anne Gaskins Packard, a widow, and together the couple would have three daughters and two sons.

"Burnt House Field," Lee Family Estate, in Coles Point, Virginia (photo by Lawrence Knorr).

In 1773, Richard Lee was a member of the Virginia Committee of Correspondence along with Peyton Randolph, Robert Carter Nicholas, Richard Bland, Benjamin Harrison, Edmund Pendleton, Patrick Henry, Dudley Digges, Dabney Carr, Archibald Cary, and Thomas Jefferson. The following year, Lee was elected to the Continental Congress where he served until May 1779. During this time, Lee was a signer of the Continental Association, the Declaration of Independence, and the Articles of Confederation.

Regarding independence, Lee was an early and ardent proponent. Following Lexington and Concord, he was still in the minority, but as time went by, more and more delegates joined him. On June 7, 1776, Lee put forth a motion for independence,

> Resolved: That these United Colonies are, and of right ought to be, free and independent States, that they are absolved from all allegiance to the British Crown, and that all political connection between them and the State of Great Britain is, and ought to be, totally dissolved.

There was rancorous opposition to the motion, so much so that the President of Congress, John Hancock, had to table it to avoid a fight. Meanwhile, the Committee of Five including Thomas Jefferson, Ben Franklin, John Adams, Roger Sherman, and Robert Livingston set about drafting a formal declaration. Though absent on July 4th, Richard and his brother Francis returned in August to sign the document, being the only brothers to do so.

Soon after, Lee was accused by John Hancock and Robert Morris of conspiring with John and Samuel Adams to remove Washington as commander of the Continental Army. At this time his brother Arthur Lee was serving as a diplomat to France along with Benjamin Franklin and Silas Deane. Arthur informed Richard that Deane was using the position for his own personal gain. Richard took to the floor of the Congress and denounced Deane and moved to recall him from Paris. Deane did so and defended himself before Congress, causing a rift in the body. This forced Henry Laurens to resign as the President of Congress. In retaliation, Deane accused the entire Lee family of corruption. Lee's friend, John Adams, wrote to Samuel Cooper in February 1779 a defense of the Lee family,

> The complaint against the family of Lees is a very extraordinary thing indeed. I am no idolater of that family or any other, but I

> believe their greatest fault is having more men of merit in it than any other family; and if that family fails the American cause, or grows unpopular among their fellow-citizens, I know not what family or what person will stand the test.

Lee soon resigned from his seat in the Congress and returned to Virginia where he continued to serve in the state House of Delegates and as a colonel in the Westmoreland militia.

In 1784, Colonel Arthur Campbell wrote to encourage Lee to reconsider service in the Continental Congress. He did so and was elected in June 1784. At that point, Thomas Mifflin resigned as President of Congress and the position was vacant for several months. In November, Lee agreed to take the position and held it until November 1785 when he was succeeded by John Hancock. During his tenure, the U.S. dollar was established as the currency of the land, tied to the Spanish dollar (piece of eight). The

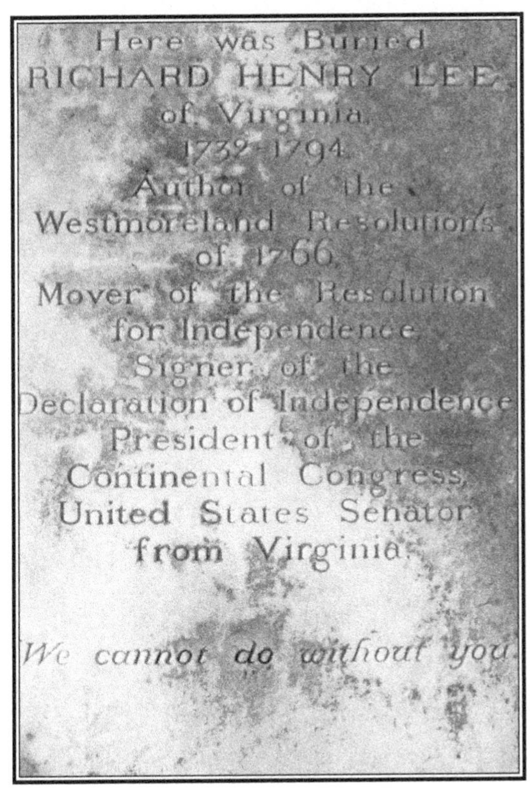

Detail from Richard Henry Lee's gravestone (photo by Lawrence Knorr).

Congress also unsuccessfully worked to sell western lands to cover the war debts.

Lee was a delegate to the Virginia convention to ratify the U.S. Constitution in 1788 and was one of two senators appointed to serve in the first Congress. He did so from March 1789 until he resigned in October 1792 as his health was beginning to fail.

Richard Henry Lee died on June 19, 1794, at the age of 62. Lee was buried at the Lee family estate's graveyard at "Burnt House Field," in Coles Point, Virginia. His gravestone reads,

> Here was buried Richard Henry Lee, of Virginia, 1732-1794. Author of the Westmoreland Resolutions of 1766. Mover of the Resolution for Independence. Signer of the Declaration of Independence. President of the Continental Congress. United States Senator from Virginia.

Many public schools across the nation are named after Lee. In 1941, a liberty ship bore his name.

Philip Livingston
(1716–1778)

Died in York

Buried at Prospect Hill Cemetery,
York, Pennsylvania.

Continental Association • Declaration of Independence

Philip Livingston opposed violence and once said that independence was "a vain shallow and ridiculous project" and warned that America would collapse if separated from England.

On his first trip out of Massachusetts, John Adams was on his way to Philadelphia to serve as a member of the Continental Congress. On a stop in New York, he was able to arrange meetings with some of New York's representatives that would serve in Congress with him. Among these was Philip Livingston. Adams found that Livingston not only opposed revolution but that he distrusted New Englanders. Livingston questioned Adams as to why Massachusetts had once hanged Quakers and used the incident to argue that a revolution would only result in the colonies fighting each other. Adams later said that it was impossible to reason with Livingston. However, the behavior of the British government eventually turned the New Yorker into an ardent patriot and an active promoter of efforts to raise and fund troops for the war.

Livingston was born on January 15, 1716, in Albany, New York into a prosperous family. His father Robert Livingston had emigrated to America from Scotland in 1673. He settled in Albany and quickly established himself in the fur trade. In 1687 the English Royal Governor granted him ownership of a tract of land consisting of 160,000 acres on the east bank of the Hudson River. The land became known as the "Manor of Livingston" and remains in the family to the present day.

Portrait of Philip Livingston by Pompeo Girolamo Batoni, circa 1783.

Robert saw to it that young Philip was tutored at home and then attended and graduated from Yale University in 1737. After marrying Christina Broeck, the daughter of the mayor of Albany, the couple settled in New York City where he became a very successful merchant and took an active part in civic affairs. His accomplishments during this time included pushing for the founding of Kings College (known today as Columbia University), the establishment of a Professorship of Divinity at Yale, the building of the first meeting house for the Methodist Society in America, and providing aid to organize the New York Public Library. In 1754 he was elected an alderman in the City, his first venture into public life. He would continue to be elected alderman for nine consecutive years. His success in these elections suggests that he was perceived as an effective representative by those who were able to cast ballots. In 1758 he was also elected to the Colonial Legislature and would urge moderation in dealings with England.

In 1765 he attended the Stamp Act Congress which produced the first formal protest to the Crown. In July 1775, he signed The Olive Branch Petition, a final attempt to achieve an understanding with the Crown. The petition appealed directly to King George III to cease hostilities and restore harmony. The King refused to respond to the plea and proclaimed the Colonies to be in a state of rebellion. Livingston was elected to the First and Second Continental Congress and during this time he changed his mind and supported the Revolution and signed the Declaration of Independence in 1776. He accepted independence reluctantly, dreading the social upheaval.

In September 1775, he was one of nine men appointed to the Secret Committee—later known as the Committee on Commerce—charged with arranging the importation of arms and gunpowder for the patriot forces He remained a member throughout his time in Congress and spent a large part of his own money to purchase supplies for the army. When the British army captured New York City, they seized his two houses forcing his family to flee to Kingston. They used his Duke Street home as a barracks and his Brooklyn Heights residence as a Royal Navy Hospital.

Unfortunately, Livingston did not live to see the American victory. He was elected to Congress in October 1777. During this particularly critical and gloomy period in the Revolution, Congress was forced to meet in York, Pennsylvania because the British had seized Philadelphia. Livingston's health was precarious, as he was diagnosed with dropsy in the chest (today it would be called congestive heart failure) with no rational prospect of recovery or improvement. Yet his love of his country was unwavering, and so he did not hesitate to give up the comforts of home and family.

Grave of Philip Livingston at Prospect Hill Cemetery, York, Pennsylvania (photo by Joe Farley).

With his health declining, he made the trip to York after

bidding his friends and family a final farewell. He believed he would never return. He proved to be correct; on June 12, 1778, Philip Livingston died. He was sixty-two years old. The entire Congress attended his funeral and declared a mourning period of a month. He was first buried in a churchyard at the German Reformed Church on West Market Street in York but later moved to Prospect Hill Cemetery in York. In 2005, Descendants of the Signers of the Declaration of Independence honored him by attaching a plaque to his tombstone identifying him as a Signer of the Declaration. A number of the direct descendants took part in the dedication ceremony.

Arthur Middleton
(1742–1787)
Defender of Charleston

Buried at the gardens at "Middleton Place,"
Charleston, South Carolina.

Declaration of Independence • Military

Arthur Middleton was a signer of the Declaration of Independence and, along with his father, Henry, was a delegate to the Continental Congress (1776-77 and 1781-82). A wealthy plantation owner, Arthur was also a leading attorney in colonial South Carolina.

Arthur was born at "Middleton Place," his father's expansive estate along the Ashley River west of Charleston, South Carolina, on June 26, 1742. He was the son of Henry Middleton and Mary Baker Williams, both of English descent. Father Henry owned, at one point, 20 plantations comprising approximately 50,000 acres, worked by over 800 slaves.

Young Arthur was first taught by private tutors and schools in the Charleston area before traveling to England to attend Hackney (later Harrow), Westminster School, and Trinity Hall, Cambridge University, where he graduated in 1760 at the age of 18. He then studied law at the Middle Temple in London, before touring Europe for two years, acquiring a taste for music, painting, sculpture, and architecture. He enjoyed a prolonged stay in Rome, appreciating its ancient heritage. He returned home just before Christmas 1763, a well-educated and cultured Renaissance man.

On August 19, 1764, Middleton married Mary Izard, the daughter of his neighbor, Walter Izard, a plantation owner and captain of a Berkeley regiment in 1712 who also served in the Yemassee War. The young couple settled in at "Middleton Place" and produced nine children.

Portrait of Arthur Middleton from the detail from a 1771 family portrait of the Middleton Family. The full portrait depicts Arthur; his wife Mary Izard Middleton, and their infant son Henry. It was painted by Benjamin West.

During his 20s, Arthur engaged in planting and became a justice of the peace Berkeley County in 1765 followed by election to the South Carolina House of Commons from 1765 to 1768 and again from 1772 to 1775.

Vehemently anti-Loyalist, Arthur was a member of the American Party in Carolina, a founding member of the Council of Safety in 1775 and 1776 (including its Secret Committee), and a delegate to the South Carolina Congress when it created its state constitution in 1776. Middleton wrote to William Henry Drayton on April 15, 1775:

> You put me in mind of Cicero Parthians after the Surrender of Pindenissum. You may say with him 'take it however as a

> Certainty, that no one could do more than I have done with such an Army." I hope you will do great matters with your great Guns, & I wish your Second in Command was not quite so sleepy, it is pity you had not roused him with a discharge. If you should not find it hot enough up your way, pray hasten down for in all probability we shall have warm work here 'ere long. It is confidently said Transports & Frigates will be here soon. Col. Laurens writes you & I suppose will acquaint you with our late Transactions. Fort Johnson is in our hands, & garrisoned with 150 men, which will be reinforc'd this night.

Said Benjamin Rush of Middleton, "he was a man of cynical temper but upright intentions towards his country." Others described him, variously, as being middle-sized, well-formed with great muscular strength and fine features expressive of firmness and decision, a celebrated, capricious aristocrat but like his forbears very public-spirited. Middleton had great disdain for Loyalists and assisted in the confiscation of the estates of those who had fled the country. He also participated in the tarring and feathering of those who remained.

Middleton succeeded his father when elected to the Continental Congress from 1776 to 1777 during which he proudly signed the Declaration of Independence. He served again in the Congress from 1781 to 1782. This entire time, from 1776 through 1786, he was also a justice of the peace in South Carolina.

During the Revolution, Middleton served as an officer in the local militia in the defense of Charleston. As the British scoured the countryside, they plundered plantations, grabbing anything that they could carry. The Middletons fled to Charleston ahead of the troops. During this time, the British plundered his estate including over 200 slaves, which were sold in the West Indies. After the city's fall to the British in 1780, he was a prisoner, along with Edward Rutledge and Thomas Heyward, Jr., from May 1780 to July 1781 in St. Augustine, Florida, until exchanged. Wife Mary begged, to no avail, for help from the British to care for her nine children.

During his imprisonment, Arthur was again elected to the Continental Congress. He was reelected on 4 October 4, 1781, and again on January 31, 1782. A note from Daniel of St. Thomas Jenifer to John Hall, July 24, 1781, mentioned the freed patriots,

The rebuilt "Middleton Place" as it looks today (photo by Lawrence Knorr).

"Ned [sic] Rutledge, Middleton, and Gadsden with many others exchanged are dayly [sic] expected from Augustine."

Middleton left the Congress before his term was out and returned home to "Middleton Place" where he focused on restoring his plantation and South Carolina affairs. Governor John Rutledge, the brother of his cellmate Edward Rutledge, appointed him to the state senate. He was re-elected to the seat in 1782. He was a member of the privy council that year and subsequently a member of the state house of representatives in 1785 and 1786. He was also a member of the board of trustees of Charleston College.

Middleton passed away suddenly on January 1, 1787, at the age of 44 at one of the Middleton plantations, "The Oaks." He was interred in the family mausoleum in the gardens at "Middleton Place," near Charleston, South Carolina, where he rests to this day. The *State Gazette of South Carolina* of January 4, 1787, included a notice about Middleton, describing him as a "tender husband and parent, humane master, steady unshaken patriot, the gentleman, and the scholar." He left behind a wife, eight children, "an untarnished name," and 600 slaves.

Historian Alexander Garden wrote in 1828:

> I know no man, whose exemplary conduct, throughout the whole progress of the Revolution, deserves more gratefully to be remembered, than that of Arthur Middleton. Possessed of ample fortune, and endowed with talents of the highest order, improved

> by study, and refined by traveling, he devoted himself with decision to the service of his country . . . He, on all occasions, advocated the most vigorous measures, clearly evincing that he was not one of those, who shrunk in times of danger from responsibility. Frank and open to temper, he freely uttered the bold conceptions of his ardent spirit, censuring with indignant pride the cautious policy of the timid and irresolute, and expressing the highest indignation at the arts of the designing.

Among Middleton's heirs included his son Henry Middleton (1770-1846), who served as Governor of South Carolina (1810-12), in the U.S. House of Representatives (1815-19), and as U.S. minister to Russia (1820-30), and his daughter Emma Philadelphia Middleton (1776-1813), who married U.S. Senator Ralph Izard (1741/42-1804). His grandson, Williams Middleton (1809-1883), signed the Ordinance of Secession that separated South Carolina from the Union and launched the American Civil War in 1861. Arthur Middleton's son-in-law was Congressman Daniel Elliott Huger who was the grandfather-in-law of Confederate General Arthur Middleton Manigault who was also a descendant of Henry Middleton. Arthur Middleton was also an ancestor of actor Charles

The grave of Arthur Middleton in the lovely gardens at "Middleton Place" near Charleston, South Carolina (photo by Lawrence Knorr).

B. Middleton, who played Ming the Merciless in the Flash Gordon movies of the 1930s.

The plantation passed to Henry, his eldest son, but it was burned and pillaged by Union troops during the Civil War. Today, “Middleton Place” is a historic landmark. A mansion was rebuilt and the grounds, including the Middleton gardens, are open to the public.

Arthur Middleton has been remembered in other ways. The United States Navy ship, USS *Arthur Middleton* (AP-55/APA-25), was named for him. Middleton’s signature and those of all the signers of the Declaration of Independence are carved on granite rocks in a lagoon near the Washington Monument. The famous Trumbull painting “The Declaration of Independence” hangs in the U.S. Capitol. The figure of Arthur Middleton is shown standing in a group of five delegates on the left side of the painting, on the extreme right of the group, with his head tilted forward.

Henry Middleton
(1717–1784)

President of Congress

Buried at St. James Goose Creek Cemetery,
Goose Creek, South Carolina.

Continental Association • President of Congress

Henry Middleton was a signer of the Continental Association during his service in the Continental Congress from 1774-1776 as a delegate from South Carolina. He also briefly served as the second President of Congress. Middleton was a wealthy plantation owner and the father of Declaration of Independence signer Arthur Middleton. However, after the fall of Charleston in 1780, he reaffirmed his loyalty to the king and remained a British subject until his death in 1784.

Middleton was born on his father Arthur Middleton's plantation, "The Oakes" near Charleston, South Carolina, in 1717. He was the son of Arthur and Sarah (née Amory) Middleton. The Middleton line had likely originated near Derbyshire, England, as far back as Queen Elizabeth I. Arthur (the elder) served in the colonial government including rising to acting governor. Middleton was likely taught by private tutors at home before going to England to complete his education.

During his younger years, Middleton served as a justice of the peace and later was elected to the colonial Commons of the Hour of Assembly, representing his St. George's County. In 1754, he was elected Speaker of this body and was later named as a member of His Majesty's Council for the Province of South Carolina.

Middleton married Mary Baker Williams with whom he had a dozen children, seven of whom survived childhood. Upon marrying Mary Williams in 1741, the daughter of John Williams, also

Portrait of Henry Middleton by Benjamin West, circa 1771.

a wealthy plantation owner, Middleton received a dowry which included the plantation that would become "Middleton Place." He and the family lived there until Mary's death in 1761, at which time he moved back to "The Oakes" and gave "Middleton Place" to his son Arthur. After Mary died, he married Mary Henrietta Bull, the daughter of William Bull, who had been the Lieutenant Governor of South Carolina. She died in 1772. The two had no children together, Middleton last married Lady Mary McKenzie in 1776.

Early on, Middleton was against the Stamp Act, and by 1770 had declined to continue serving on His Majesty's Council. In 1774, he was elected to the first Continental Congress, representing South Carolina along with John Rutledge, Christopher Gadsden, Thomas Lynch, and Edward Rutledge, Middleton attended the entire first Continental Congress and into the second, until early 1776 when he became ill and was replaced by his son Arthur. Middleton had also been elected President of Congress for a brief period, October 22 to 26, in 1775 while Peyton Randolph was unable to serve. However, some records seem to indicate he might have served longer, starting earlier in October. A petition to Ben Franklin and others had been signed by Middleton, as President of Congress, as early as October 6.

During his service, Middleton had been instrumental in establishing a new government for South Carolina and was well-respected by others for his willingness to negotiate with the King as opposed to leaping right to independence like others from the northern colonies. In this regard, he differed from his son, who was a staunch voice for independence. Middleton resigned from his position in the Congress and returned to "The Oakes" prior to the Declaration of Independence due to declining health. His son signed the document instead.

As one of the leaders of the revolt against British rule, Middleton came to the attention to the British authorities, who ordered his arrest and execution. From a letter from the Earl of Dunmore from London, 30 January 1775:

> From unquestionable authority I learn, that about a fortnight ago, dispatches were sent hence by a sloop of war to General [Thomas] Gage, containing, among other things, a Royal Proclamation, declaring the inhabitants of Massachusetts Bay and some others, in the different Colonies, actual rebels; with a blank commission to try and execute such of them as he can hold of . . . with this is sent a list of names, to be inserted in the commission as he may judge expedient. I do not know them all, but Messrs. Samuel Adams, John Adams, Robert Treat Paine, and John Hancock, of Massachusetts Bay; John Dickinson, of Philadelphia; Peyton Randolph, of Virginia, and Henry Middleton, of South Carolina, are particularly named, with many others. This blacklist, the General will, no doubt, keep to himself, and unfold it gradually, as he finds it convenient.

Back in South Carolina, during the period between royal rule and statehood, Middleton was a member of the state Legislative Council, which helped to form South Carolina. In 1778 he was elected to the South Carolina state Senate, where he served until 1780.

When Charleston fell to the British in 1780, Middleton was faced with financial ruin and certain execution. Rather than face such an end, he paid off the British invaders and reaffirmed his loyalty. Subsequently, his estates were not further touched, though his son's was burned to the ground and ransacked.

Middleton's health continued to decline over the following years. He died in Charleston on June 13, 1784, after a long illness. He was laid to rest at St. James Goose Creek cemetery at "Goose Creek," one of the Middleton family estates, located in Berkeley County, South Carolina. In all, through purchases and other means, Middleton, by the time of his death, had accumulated some 50,000 acres of land, a total of 50 estates and plantations, and approximately 800 slaves, becoming one of the wealthiest men in South Carolina prior to and during the American Revolution.

Apparently, his reversal of loyalty did not diminish the opinions held of him locally due to his many contributions early in the fight for independence and the role played by his son, Arthur. His estates were not confiscated as were many loyalists following the war.

The graves of Henry Middleton's daughter Susannah Middleton and her husband Continental Congressman John Parker at St. James Goose Creek Cemetery in Goose Creek, South Carolina. The location of Henry's grave is not known, but it may be close to this one. Based on the old etching, there was a tombstone next to it that no longer exists. (photo by Lawrence Knorr).

Thomas Mifflin
(1744–1800)
Governor Mifflin

Buried at Trinity Lutheran Church,
Lancaster, Pennsylvania.

Continental Association • U.S. Constitution • Military
President of Congress • First Governor of Pennsylvania

Thomas Mifflin is a Founding Father of our country whose contributions have gone unheralded and are largely forgotten. He risked his life for American independence and democracy. He spent almost his entire life in public service. He was expelled from his church for fighting the British, served as President of the Continental Congress, was a signer of the U.S. Constitution, and was Pennsylvania's first governor. Despite his many accomplishments and his contributions as a Founding Father, there is no monument that identifies his grave. There is a roadside historical marker saying he is interred somewhere on the grounds of Trinity Lutheran Church. It is uncertain where precisely he is buried. In addition, there is little mention of his many distinguished accomplishments during his long life of service to his country and his state. One internet site claims the grave was paved over for a parking lot. There is a marble slab in the wall of the church that states he was a signer of the Constitution.

Thomas Mifflin was born on January 10, 1744, in Philadelphia where his parents were prominent Quakers. He attended local schools and in 1760, graduated from the College of Philadelphia (today known as the University of Pennsylvania). He went into business with a local merchant and in 1765, he formed a partnership in the import and export business with his younger brother.

Portrait of Thomas Mifflin, 1773, by John Singleton Copley.

Mifflin married a distant cousin, Sarah Morris, in 1771. That same year, he was elected city warden. In 1772, he began the first of four consecutive terms in the Colonial legislature. In the summer of 1774, Mifflin was elected by the legislature to the First Continental Congress. His work there spread his reputation across America and led to his election to the Second Continental Congress which convened in Philadelphia in the aftermath of the fighting at Lexington and Concord.

He played a major role in the creation of Philadelphia's militia and was commissioned as a major in May 1775. Despite his family being Quakers for generations, he was expelled from the church because military service violated the pacifist nature of the faith. In what had to be a difficult decision Mifflin viewed service to his country as more important than adherence to religious beliefs.

When Congress created the Continental Army in June 1775, Mifflin resigned from the militia to go on active duty with the regulars. George Washington, the Commander in Chief, selected Mifflin as one of his aides. Shortly after, Washington appointed him Quartermaster General of the Continental Army. His service as Quartermaster earned him a promotion to Brigadier General, but he longed for a field command and requested to be reassigned. He was transferred to the infantry and led a brigade of Pennsylvania continentals during the New York City campaign. He fought bravely in the battles of Long Island, Trenton, and Princeton, and was with Washington during the terrible winter at Valley Forge. Throughout this time his persuasive oratory convinced many men not to leave the military service. However, he was soon returned to the position of Quartermaster when no suitable replacement could be found for him. It was a move that left him bitterly disappointed.

In November 1776, General Mifflin was sent by Washington to Philadelphia to report to the Continental Congress on the critical condition of the army. The Continental Army was outgunned and outmanned and unable to make a stand in New Jersey to stop the advancing British march towards Philadelphia. It was a wise move by the Commander-in-Chief to send General Mifflin to rally Philadelphia, as Congress, in fear of losing the capital was preparing to take flight to Baltimore. When the Continental army was forced into Pennsylvania, the citizens of Philadelphia began to panic. Business was suspended, schools were closed, and roads leading from the city were crowded with refugees all fleeing the city.

At a town meeting, General Mifflin addressed the crowd and much of the Continental Congress. After listening to Mifflin, Congress formally appealed to the militia of Philadelphia and surrounding areas to join Washington's army. Mifflin organized and trained three regiments of militia and sent 1,500 men to Washington. He also orchestrated a re-supply of Washington's desperate troops once they reached Valley Forge. These were critical components needed by Washington to cross the Delaware and attack the British in Trenton. In recognition of his services, Congress commissioned Mifflin as a major-general and made him a member of the Board of War.

On the Board of War, General Mifflin joined a growing number of delegates and generals who shared the dissatisfaction of General Washington's conduct of the war. He sympathized with the views of General Horatio Gates and General Thomas Conway who blamed Washington for the losses of the Continental Army. In the fall of 1777, Horatio Gates, with the help of Benedict Arnold, defeated the British forces at Saratoga. Almost immediately, Washington's enemies, emboldened by the victory, sought his replacement with the "Hero of Saratoga" General Gates. General Conway organized an effort to have the Board of War establish Gates as the new Commander-in-Chief. This became known as "The Conway Cabal." When the effort failed, Mifflin submitted his resignation. Congress refused to accept it, but he was discharged from the Board of War.

In late 1778, while still on active duty, he won re-election to the State Legislature. In 1780, he was again elected to the Continental Congress and in 1783, the Continental Congress elected him as President of the Congress. He presided over the ratification of the Treaty of Paris, which ended the Revolution and ironically accepted Washington's formal resignation as Commander-in-Chief. In what many historians say was one of the most remarkable events of United States history George Washington was formally received by President Thomas Mifflin and Congress. At the pinnacle of his power and popularity, Washington resigned his commission as Commander-in-Chief to the President of the Continental Congress, a man who had once conspired to replace him.

Plaque honoring Thomas Mifflin on the street-side of Trinity Lutheran Churchyard in Lancaster, Pennsylvania (photo by Joe Farrell).

Mifflin represented Pennsylvania at the United States Constitutional Convention and was a signer of it. He presided over the committee that wrote Pennsylvania's first constitution which established a bicameral legislature with a strong governor. He then ran for governor in 1790 and was elected as Pennsylvania's first governor by a margin of almost ten to one. He served three terms as governor until 1799.

Thomas Mifflin died on January 20, 1800, in Lancaster and was buried in the cemetery of Trinity Lutheran Church at state expense since his estate was too small to cover funeral costs. The cemetery no longer exists. Most of the bodies were moved in the 1840s to Woodward Hill Cemetery, but Mifflin's was not. There is a historical marker on South Duke Street that says, "here are interred the remains of Thomas Wharton, Jr. and Governor Thomas Mifflin."

Robert Morris
(1734–1806)
Revolutionary Financier

Buried at Christ Episcopal Church and Churchyard,
Philadelphia, Pennsylvania.

Declaration of Independence • Articles of Confederation
U.S. Constitution • Finance

This Founder was once considered the wealthiest man in the country. He gave of his wealth willingly for the Revolution he helped bring about during his service in the Continental Congress. His signature can be found on the Declaration of Independence, the Articles of Confederation, and the United States Constitution. Along with George Washington and Benjamin Franklin, he is still widely viewed as one of the three men who made American Independence possible. He is also regarded as one of the founders of the financial system of the United States. For three years he served as the Superintendent of Finance, a time during which he was the central civilian in the government and considered by many to be, next to George Washington, the most powerful man in the country. He represented Pennsylvania in the United States Senate. Despite his widely successful career in business he spent over three years in debtor's prison and passed away in poverty. His name was Robert Morris.

Morris was born in Liverpool, England on January 20, 1734. His father was an ironmonger in Liverpool prior to emigrating to America to establish a tobacco shipping company in Oxford, Maryland. This business proved successful and when Morris reached the age of 13 he joined his father in America. In 1750 the elder Morris took a small boat in order to board a ship called the *Liverpool Merchant* to follow the custom of welcoming the captain

Oil on canvas painting of Robert Morris by Robert Edge Pine, circa 1785

to America. That task completed, he climbed back into the little boat to return to shore. The captain, also following the custom at the time, readied the ship's cannon to fire a salute. An insect, possibly a fly, landed on the captain's nose and he raised his arm to chase it away. The crew viewed this action as a signal to fire the cannon which they did prematurely. Morris, Sr., who was only 20 yards away, was struck by wadding which broke his right arm. The wound developed an infection and he died six days later leaving his considerable fortune to his son.

The suddenly wealthy Morris had been educated in Philadelphia where he became an apprentice to a merchant and mayor of the city, Charles Willing. The mayor died in 1854 and his son made Morris a partner in the firm. In 1757 the two young businessmen formed a shipping and banking firm. They would remain partners until 1779.

In 1769 at the age of 35, Morris married the 20-year-old Mary White. The couple would produce seven children; five sons, and two daughters. White came from a well-respected Maryland family. Her brother, William White, was a well known Episcopal Bishop. Morris worshipped at St. Peters Church in Philadelphia which was run by his brother in law. When the Continental Congress was in session many of its members also worshipped there.

As a leading merchant in one of America's most important cities, Morris could not escape the political issues of the day. Though he did not believe the time was right for independence, he took the side of the colonies in the struggle with England. In 1774 he signed on to boycott the importation of British goods despite the damage it would do to his business.

In 1775 Morris was appointed to the Continental Congress. Here he put his business experience to work for the American cause. As a member of the committee for commerce, he worked to supply the Continental Army with supplies by paying for them with shipments of American goods. Still, as of July 1, 1776, he wasn't ready to vote for American independence. On that day he cast a preliminary vote opposing separating from England.

On July 2, 1776, when the official vote was taken he abstained so that Pennsylvania would not be the only colony that failed to support the measure. Once the measure was passed, he became an ardent supporter of American independence and on August 2, 1776, he signed the Declaration of Independence. Regarding this act, he said, "I am not one of those politicians that run testy when my own plans are not adopted. I think it is the duty of a good citizen to follow when he cannot lead."

There are numerous examples of the work Morris did that earned him the title "Financer of the Revolution." One of the most important of these occurred after Washington crossed the Delaware on his way to victory in the Battle of Trenton. As General Howe's British and German Hessian troops retreated, the American general was being urged to pursue and strike the enemy in order to capitalize on his recent victory. Washington's problem was that his battle-hardened New England recruits' enlistments were ending and they were due to go home. Washington sent a messenger to Morris asking him to gather enough money to pay each soldier a ten dollar bonus for extending their enlistment for six weeks. Since Washington wanted the funds to return with the messenger, Morris immediately went to work using his own funds and his own credit to fulfill Washington's request. In addition, Morris had heard that the general was also low on wine so in addition to the requested funds he sent along a quarter cask of good vintage. Using the funds Morris provided, Washington was able to keep the New Englanders in the army. It seemed that every time Washington was short on cash, Morris was able to find it. It has been reported that Morris gave one million of his own money to fund the decisive Yorktown campaign.

By the time the Revolution ended, Morris had already signed the Articles of Confederation creating a loose and ineffective union of the thirteen former colonies. In 1781 Congress named him the Superintendent of Finance. Only days after taking this position, Morris proposed the establishment of a national bank. The Bank of North America was the first financial institution chartered by the United States. The funding for the bank came, in part, through a loan from France which Morris had worked to obtain. He served as the Superintendent until 1784.

In 1787 Morris was one of Pennsylvania's representatives at the Constitutional Convention meeting in Philadelphia. On May 13th of that year Morris, now considered the richest man in the country, welcomed his old friend General Washington to Philadelphia and walked with him to his temporary residence where the General settled in comfortably in one of the city's grand mansions. On May 25th it was Morris who nominated Washington to be the President of the Convention. Though he attended the Constitutional Convention regularly, his participation was rare in that he spoke only twice and one of those occasions was nominating Washington. When the convention concluded, he added his name to the Constitution and worked for its ratification.

Some historians say that Washington wanted Morris to be the first Secretary of the Treasury but that the Pennsylvanian declined and recommended Alexander Hamilton who supported many of the policies that Morris had championed as the Superintendent of Finance. Morris was elected to the Senate and served in the first Congress. As a senator, he supported the Federalist agenda and strongly backed Hamilton's financial proposals. When some of his fellow members of that initial Congress expressed their frustration at what they viewed as slowness and inefficiency of the new government in accomplishing tasks, Morris disagreed. Older than many of his peers, Morris stated, "I have so often seen good consequences arise from public debate and discussion that I am not amongst the number of those who complain of the delay."

Morris, like several other Founders, was heavily involved in land speculation schemes. Unfortunately, in his case, a number were unsuccessful and he found himself unable to sell his western properties or pay the taxes on them. Many of those who witnessed the spectacular rise of Morris to the wealthiest man on the continent now watched a fall that was no less spectacular. Hounded by his creditors he was arrested and placed in a Philadelphia debtors' prison from February 1798 to August of 1801. In 1946 the *Harrisburg Evening News* reported that a review of his papers showed that Morris paid $1.25 a week for his board in his cell during his stay there. In 1800 Congress passed the temporary Bankruptcy Act which once enacted resulted in his release. The act was passed, at least in part to get Morris out of prison.

After his release, Morris was in ill health and was cared for by his wife for the rest of his days. He passed away May 8, 1806, and was laid to rest in the family vault of his brother in law Bishop William White in what is now the Christ Episcopal Church and Churchyard in Philadelphia. If you visit you will see a plaque placed by the Pennsylvania Constitution Commemorative Committee that notes his service during the Constitutional Convention. There is clearly far more to the story of this Founder who went from being the richest man in America to a Founder who, according to an April 19, 1939 article in the *Pittsburgh Post Gazette*, submitted "with patience and fortitude" to poverty.

Grave of Robert Morris at Christ Episcopal Church & Churchyard in Philadelphia, Pennsylvania (photo by Joe Farley).

John Morton
(1724–1777)

Pennsylvania's Swing Vote

Buried at St. Paul's Burying Ground,
Chester, Pennsylvania.

Continental Association • Declaration of Independence

John Morton was an important Founding Father of the United States. He was elected to both the First and Second Continental Congress and was a signatory to the Continental Association and the U.S. Declaration of Independence. He provided the swing vote that allowed Pennsylvania to vote in favor of independence.

He was born in 1724 in Ridley Township, Pennsylvania. His father died just before he was born and not much is known about his childhood, not even the month or day of his birth. Both sides of his family emigrated from Sweden or Finland. His mother remarried an Englishman, John Sketchley, who played an important role in his development. He attended formal school for only about 3 months but thanks to his stepfather he would grow up to be a farmer, a surveyor, a lawyer, and a judge.

In 1748, Morton married Ann Justis. The couple had nine children and was active in the Anglican Church in Chester County. His public service began in 1756 when he was elected to the Pennsylvania Assembly. The next year he was also appointed justice of the peace, an office he held until 1764. He was one of four Pennsylvania delegates to the Stamp Act Congress in 1765. This congress is generally viewed as one of the first organized and coordinated political actions of the American Revolution. It was the first gathering of elected representatives from the colonies to devise a unified protest against new British taxation.

Portrait of John Morton from of painting of doubtful origin, circa 1868

In 1766, after ten years of service in the Pennsylvania Assembly, Morton gave up his seat to become the sheriff of Chester County. He was appointed sheriff after the incumbent sheriff, his close friend, died. He was reelected sheriff in 1767 and again in 1768. In 1769 he gave up the sheriff position and returned to the Pennsylvania Assembly. In 1774 he was elected Speaker of the Pennsylvania Assembly and elected to be a delegate to the First Continental Congress in Philadelphia. It was in October of that year when Congress formed the Continental Association. The Association signified the increasing cooperation between the colonies. As a sign of the desire still prevalent at the time, to avoid open revolution, the Association notably opened with a profession of allegiance to the king, and they placed the blame for " a ruinous system of colony administration" upon Parliament. The result called for implementing a trade boycott of Great Britain. Congress hoped that by imposing economic sanctions, they would pressure Great Britain into redressing the grievances of the colonies, in particular repealing the Intolerable Acts passed by the British Parliament. The Association aimed to alter Britain's policies towards the colonies without severing allegiance. Morton was one of seven Pennsylvania delegates to sign.

The next year he was again elected to the Second Continental Congress where he played a key role. As the Congress moved toward declaring independence, the Pennsylvania delegation was divided. Pennsylvania was considered a crucial state in this effort. Morton was undecided as the vote was approaching. Benjamin Franklin and James Wilson were aye votes. Thomas Willing and Charles Humphreys were nays. When Morton decided to vote aye on July 2, two other delegates, John Dickinson and Robert Morris chose to absent themselves and thus Pennsylvania cast its vote for independence. He signed the historic document on August 2 with most of the other delegates. As a result of this vote, many friends, relatives, and neighbors turned against him.

Later that year Morton became Chairman of the Committee of The Whole and was heavily involved in writing the Articles of Confederation, the new nation's first form of government. In early 1777 he became very ill with what is suspected to have been tuberculosis and died on April 1. He was the first signer of the Declaration of Independence to die.

He was buried in Old St. Paul's Burial Ground also known as the Old Swedish Burial Ground, in the city of Chester, Pennsylvania. His grave remained unmarked until October 1845, when the present obelisk was erected by his descendants. When we first visited his grave the place showed shameful signs of neglect. The grounds were badly overgrown, many of the graves deteriorated, and the flag over Morton's grave in tatters. A second visit revealed some improvement.

Grave of John Morton at Saint Paul's Burying Ground in Chester, Pennsylvania (photo by Lawrence Knorr).

William Paca
(1740–1799)
Master of Wye

Buried at "Wye House" plantation,
Queenstown, Maryland.

Continental Association • Declaration of Independence

In his time he was viewed as a handsome, fashionable, and educated gentleman who was willing to risk his life and his property for the cause of American independence. Benjamin Rush said that he was "loved and respected by all" and at all times "a sincere patriot and honest man." He signed the Declaration of Independence as a Maryland representative to the Continental Congress. One of the reasons so little is known about the man is that all his papers and diaries were lost in a fire. Born on October 31, 1740, his name was William Paca.

Paca was the second son born to John Paca and his wife Elizabeth. The family also included five daughters. Paca's father was wealthy Maryland planter and the owner of a large estate. As a result, Paca had the good fortune of receiving an excellent and well-rounded education. First he attended the Philadelphia Academy and Charity School before moving on to the College of Philadelphia (now known as the University of Pennsylvania) where he graduated with a Bachelor of Arts degree in 1759. Three years later he received a Master of Arts degree from the same institution.

With his education complete, Paca returned to Maryland and settled in Annapolis where he studied law under Stephen Bordley who was widely considered to be the finest attorney in the colony at the time. During this period, he married Mary Chew the

Portrait of William Paca by Charles Willson Peale, circa 1772

daughter of another prominent Maryland planter and in 1764 he was admitted to the Maryland provincial bar.

Two other future signers of the Declaration of Independence, Samuel Chase and Thomas Stone, were also living in Annapolis engaged in the study of law. The three young patriots became friends with Chase and Paca, in particular, earning less than stellar reputations as far as local officials loyal to the crown were concerned. On one occasion the duo decided to stage a mock execution of a law that had been recently enacted by the royal governor. After copying the law to a sheet of paper, they took it to a mock gallows where it was hanged until it was dead. They then cut it down and burned it in a coffin as a ship owned by Paca fired a cannon shot from the Chesapeake Bay to celebrate the moment. Paca and Chase were also instrumental in the formation of the Anne Arundel County chapter of the Sons of Liberty. It was through this organization that they organized and led the local opposition to the British Stamp Act of 1765.

Paca's biographers Gregory A. Stiverson and Phoebe R. Jacobsen maintain that despite these demonstrations, Paca was no mere rabble-rouser. They maintain that "Paca preferred fighting injustice and oppression by constructing finely argued newspaper essays that traced constitutional precedents and appealed to man's natural rights." This description seems in keeping with those who would work with him later in the Continental Congress and with the manner in which he led his own life.

Paca was elected to the Maryland legislature in 1771 and was appointed to represent the state as a member of the Continental Congress in 1774. With this honor and responsibility, the year also brought grief to Paca when his wife died after giving birth to their third child. He served in Congress until 1779 and during that five-year period was among those who voted in favor of American independence and signed the document proclaiming it. John Adams praised Paca relative to the debate on American independence describing him as a "deliberator" who performed "generously and nobly" during the discussions that led to the declaration.

In 1777, Paca remarried. His second wife Ann Harrison was the daughter of a wealthy and socially prominent Philadelphia merchant. This marriage was short-lived as Ann passed away in 1780 after a long illness.

Paca's contributions to the country and to Maryland did not end when he left the Continental Congress. He spent thousands of dollars supplying the troops from Maryland who fought in the Revolution. He served as Maryland's Chief Justice and as the state's Governor. During his term as Governor he worked to provide assistance to the veterans who had fought for and won America's independence. He strongly supported the Articles of Confederation and opposed the Constitution during the ratification fight on the grounds that the federal government it created was too powerful and that it contained no bill of rights. Some of his objections were used as foundations for the initial amendments to the Constitution.

Paca fathered two children out of wedlock. The mother of one of these children was a free black woman. Paca acknowledged that he was the child's father and sent her to the best schools available. This admirable conduct was said to raise more than a few eyebrows in the young country at the time.

In 1789 President Washington appointed Paca to the Federal District Court for Maryland. It was a post he held until his death at his estate on Wye Island on October 13, 1799. Paca was laid to rest on the grounds of his estate. The estate is on private property that is posted with signs to discourage trespassers. However, every July 4th there is a wreath-laying ceremony held at Paca's grave that is often attended by his descendants.

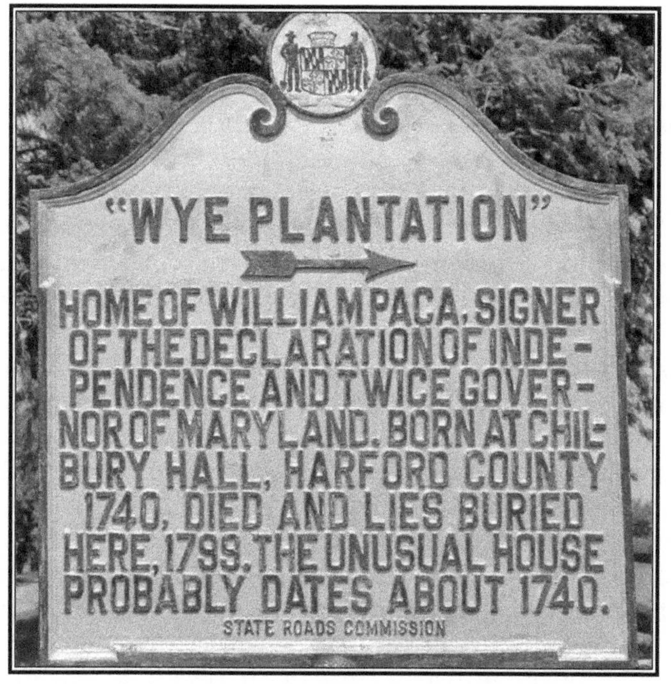

Historic marker about William Paca's "Wye House" plantation in Queen Anne County, Maryland, which is private property (photo by Lawrence Knorr).

John Penn
(1741–1788)

The Penn with a Pen

Buried at Guilford Courthouse National Military Park,
Greensboro, North Carolina.

Declaration of Independence • Articles of Confederation

Though born and raised in Virginia this Founder represented North Carolina in the Continental Congress. His chief contribution to the cause of American independence was affixing his name to the document that declared it. A skilled attorney he was noted for his oratorical gifts in his practice before judges and juries. He also reasoned his way out of a duel with the President of Congress as they were on their way to the dueling ground. His name was John Penn.

Penn was born on May 17, 1741, just outside of Fredericksburg, Virginia. His father was a farmer and his mother the daughter of a county judge. It appears that Penn's father did not value education as his son only attended school for a couple of years. By the time he reached the age of 18, Penn had different ideas regarding how to make his way in the world. His cousin, Edmund Pendleton, was an attorney and Penn began borrowing books from his library which he used to teach himself to read and write. Next, he studied law under Pendleton and earned his license to practice when he was 21.

Penn would practice the law for over a decade in Virginia. During that time he married Susan Lyme and the couple would welcome three children into the world. In 1774 the Penns moved to North Carolina where he not only resumed his law practice but also developed an interest in the patriot cause. He certainly impressed the people in his adopted state as in 1775 he was elected as a representative to the second Continental Congress.

Portrait of John Penn etched by H B Hall from a drawing in the collection of Dr. F A Emmet, 1871.

It would seem that as a member of Congress, Penn was a strong supporter of American independence. Early in 1776, he wrote to Thomas Person, a brigadier general in the North Carolina militia. Penn urged Person to "encourage our people, animate them to dare to even die for their country. Our struggle I hope will not continue long, may unanimity and success crown your endeavours."

On July 2, 1776, Penn and the other North Carolina representative Joseph Hewes voted in favor of American independence. The duo along with a third representative from North Carolina, William Hooper, who had been absent the day of the vote, signed the Declaration on August 2nd.

In 1778 Penn added his signature to the Articles of Confederation. It was during this time period that Penn found himself in multiple political arguments with Henry Laurens from South Carolina who had succeeded John Hancock as the President of Congress. Their battles reached a boiling point, at least for Laurens, and he challenged Penn to a duel to settle their differences.

Grave of John Penn at Guilford Courthouse National Military Park in Greensboro, North Carolina (photo by Lawrence Knorr).

The two would-be duelists lived in the same boarding house. The morning they were to meet on the field of honor, they sat together to eat their breakfast. Upon completing their meal, they walked together to the site chosen for the duel. Along the way, they came to a large muddy spot they needed to cross. Penn, being the younger man, proceeded to help Laurens across. During the crossing, Penn offered to let the whole matter drop and Laurens quickly agreed. They exchanged apologies and canceled the duel.

Penn left Congress in 1780 and the Governor of North Carolina, Abner Nash, promptly appointed him to his state's Board of War. Penn was an active member of the board and worked to supply war materials to Nathanael Greene's Continentals and Francis Marion's guerrillas. When the Revolution ended, he served for a short period of time as North Carolina's receiver of taxes for the Confederation government. He resigned this post because, in his view, he had not been given the authority he required to collect the taxes. He then returned to the practice of law.

Penn passed away on September 14, 1788, at the age of 47. He was laid to rest on the grounds of his home. In 1894 Penn's unmarked grave was located in a pasture marked by two large sassafras trees. According to *The Wilmington Messenger* authorities were able to find Penn's skull as well as many pieces of the walnut coffin. As reported by that paper these "sacred remains" were placed in a copper box and buried on the Guilford Battle Ground beneath a monument erected to honor North Carolina's signers. That spot marks John Penn's final resting place.

Charles Pinckney
(1757–1824)
Proponent of Slavery

Buried at St. Philip's Episcopal Church Cemetery,
Charleston, South Carolina.

U.S. Constitution • Military

Charles Pinckney was a politician from South Carolina who served in the House of Representatives, the Senate, represented South Carolina at the Constitutional Convention, and was a signer of the Constitution. He was first cousin once-removed of fellow signer Charles Cotesworth Pinckney. Times were such that Pinckney dedicated his considerable political talents to the establishment of a strong national government so that as he put it "the effects of the revolution may never cease to operate, but continue to serve as an example to others until they have unshackled all the nations that have firmness to resist the fetters of despotism." Yet, Pinckney saw slavery as a positive good and could not imagine blacks as equals. He fought for the protection of the slave trade at the Constitutional Convention and, thirty years later, opposed the Missouri Compromise because it set the dangerous precedent of allowing the federal Congress to outlaw slavery in the territories.

Charles Pinckney was born on October 26, 1757, in Charleston, South Carolina. He was the son of Charles Pinckney and Frances Brewton, members of South Carolina's social elite. Pinckney's father Colonel Pinckney was one of the colony's leading attorneys. Young Charles was tutored in Charleston in preparation for studying law in England but when the time came, his parents decided he should remain at home and study law in his father's office due to the growing unrest between the colonies and Great Britain.

Portrait of Charles Pinckney etched by Albert Rosenthal, 1888.

He started to practice law in 1779 in Charleston and about that time he enlisted in the South Carolina militia. He became a lieutenant and served at the siege of Savannah in the fall of 1779. Shortly thereafter, the British initiated a campaign resulting in the capture of Charleston in May 1780. The young lieutenant was captured and held as a prisoner until June 1781. He was confined on the prison ship *Pack Horse* in Charleston harbor. The elder Pinckney was captured and pressured to swear allegiance to the crown, which he did in order to save his estate.

After spending most of the summer of 1781 as a prisoner of war, Lieutenant Pinckney was among a group of officers exchanged through a general agreement. Upon returning home, he was elected to the Continental Congress. He first came to national prominence in May of 1786. At that time, he introduced a motion in Congress to reorganize completely the structure of the central governing body. In doing this he joined with Washington,

Hamilton, and Madison in acknowledging the weaknesses and inadequacies of the Articles of Confederation. Through Pinckney's motion, the Continental Congress established a committee, heard from the states additional calls for reform, and eventually called for a meeting of delegates from all of the states to either reform the Articles or draft an entirely new governing document.

Pinckney was chosen to represent South Carolina at the Convention in Philadelphia in 1787. His role in the convention is controversial. Although one of the youngest delegates, he later claimed to have been the most influential and contended that he had submitted a draft that was the basis of the final Constitution. This was strongly disputed by James Madison and some other framers and rejected by most historians. Historians do however recognize that he was one of the leaders, he attended full time, spoke often (over 100 times) and effectively, and contributed immensely to the final draft and to the resolution of problems that arose during the debates. His major contributions were:

- The elimination of religious testing as a qualification to office.
- The division of the legislature into House and Senate.
- The power of impeachment being granted only to the House.
- The establishment of a single chief executive, who will be called President.
- The power of raising an army and navy being granted to Congress.
- The prohibition of states to enter into a treaty or to establish interfering duties.
- The regulation of interstate and foreign commerce being controlled by the national government.

When the issue of slavery arose, Pinckney stood among his fellow southerners in defense of the institution. He openly questioned the assertion that slavery was wrong. He stated that South Carolina would reject the Constitution if the document prohibited slave importation.

He signed the Constitution in September of 1787 and returned home to marry Mary Eleanor Laurens on April 27, 1788. The couple had three children.

In 1788, he served as floor manager for the nationalist forces in the state's convention that ratified the Constitution and then

Grave of Charles Pinckney at Saint Philips Episcopal Church Cemetery in Charleston, South Carolina (photo by Lawrence Knorr).

chaired a second assembly that drafted a new state constitution along the lines laid out in Philadelphia. In between, he won the first of several terms as governor.

In 1798 Pinckney was appointed to fill an unexpired term in the United States Senate. In the presidential election of 1800, he remained loyal to Thomas Jefferson, serving as his campaign manager in South Carolina and helping to carry the state for Jefferson. The victorious Jefferson appointed Pinckney as Minister to Spain (1801-1805), in which capacity he struggled valiantly but unsuccessfully to win cession of Florida to the United States.

Charles Pinckney returned to Charleston in January 1806 and again served in the South Carolina General assembly. In December of that year, he was elected to his fourth and final term as governor. He served again in the legislature from 1810 to 1814 and then temporarily withdrew from politics. In 1818 he ran and won election to the U.S. House of Representatives where he fought against the Missouri Compromise as he was interested in the expansion of slavery into new territories and states.

In 1821, Pinckney's health began to fail and he retired from politics. He died on October 29, 1824, just three days after his 67th birthday. He was buried in St. Philips Episcopal Church Cemetery in Charleston. A portion of his estate is now preserved as the Charles Pinckney National Historic Site.

Caesar Rodney
(1728–1784)

Rode for Independence

Buried at Christ Episcopal Church Cemetery (cenotaph?),
Dover, Delaware.

Continental Association • Declaration of Independence
Military

Caesar Rodney was a militia commander in the American Revolutionary War, a delegate from Delaware in both the First and Second Continental Congress, and a signer of the Declaration of Independence. He is most famous for riding on horseback for 70 miles through a storm to reach the Pennsylvania State House in time to cast the decisive Delaware vote for independence.

Rodney was born on his father's large and prosperous farm near Dover, Delaware on October 7, 1728. The farm became known as "Byfield" and was worked by many slaves. At the age of seventeen, his father died and guardianship was entrusted to a man named Nicholas Ridgely. Rodney received very little formal education. He was tormented throughout his life by asthma, and his adult years were plagued by facial cancer. He experienced expensive, painful, and futile medical treatments. He would often wear a green scarf to hide his disfigured face. The disease would eventually kill him.

He lived all his life as a bachelor and was known for his wit and humor and was very popular. He served in the Delaware Militia during the French and Indian War where he was commissioned a captain and in 1755 was elected Sheriff of Kent County and served the maximum three years allowed. This was a powerful position in that it supervised elections and chose the grand jurors that set the county tax rate. After his term as Sheriff, he

Portrait of Caesar Rodney, artist unknown.

served in a variety of government offices in Delaware. He became prominent in what was known as the Country Party and as a result, worked closely with Thomas McKean.

He began his service in the Delaware Assembly in 1762 and continued in office through 1776. Several times he served as speaker including on June 15, 1776, when the Assembly of Delaware voted to sever all ties with the British Parliament and King.

He and McKean were elected to the Stamp Act Congress in 1765 and Rodney was the leader of the Delaware Committee of Correspondence formed to communicate with other colonies. In 1769, he tried unsuccessfully to have a law passed "prohibiting the importation of slaves" into Delaware. In 1766 he was named to the Supreme Court of the colony even though he served in the Assembly. Meanwhile, Rodney served in the Continental Congress along with McKean and George Read from 1774 through 1776. As a member of the First and Second Continental Congress, he

Grave of Caesar Rodney at Christ Episcopal Church Cemetery in Dover, Delaware (photo by Lawrence Knorr).

listened intently to the debates on independence without committing himself. He even signed the Olive Branch Petition seeking reconciliation with England in 1775, but was finally convinced that Britain "was making every kind of exertion in her favor to reduce us to unconditional submission and that no hope of reconciliation on constitutional principles could possibly remain."

The busy Rodney was appointed a colonel in May of 1775 and in September of that same year he became a brigadier general and later a major general. He served in the New Jersey area during this time and was responsible for producing the required Delaware troops to General George Washington. As a member of the Council of Safety, he was unable to secure the timely response to troop equipment needs and bought the necessary items from his own pocket. This effort resulted in many letters from Washington lauding his work.

Equestrian statue of Caesar Rodney at Rodney Square in Wilmington, Delaware (photo by Lawrence Knorr).

The Continental Congress met in the spring and summer of 1776 to contemplate declaring independence from the British Crown. The Delaware delegates were Rodney, McKean, and Read. The awesome consequences of this to the country as a whole, and to the lives and fortunes of these delegates can hardly be overstated. The discussion of the resolution made by Richard Henry Lee of Virginia took several contentious weeks. Unanimous agreement eluded its supporters and a recess was declared. The Congress reconvened on July 1. Rodney, however, was in Sussex County to look into a threatened Loyalist uprising. He received word from McKean via courier that the vote on independence was the next day and that he and George Read were deadlocked. He immediately left for Philadelphia. It was an agonizing eighty-mile ride through the summer's heat, an angry thunderstorm, and torrential rain, over dirt roads choked with mud, across rickety bridges spanning swollen streams, and over slippery cobblestone streets of the towns. He was a lone rider with no time to spare. All that he had worked for hung in the balance. He rushed to vote for a resolution that might put a noose around his neck. He arrived "in his boots and spurs" just as the voting was beginning. He voted with McKean and thereby allowed Delaware to join eleven other states in voting for independence. The wording of the Declaration of Independence was approved two days later and Rodney signed it on August 2.

In 1777 Rodney was placed in charge of the post at Trenton. He was to forward troops from Trenton to Morristown as fast as possible. On February 18 of that year, Washington wrote a letter of commendation to Rodney for the job he did in Trenton. In March 1778 he was elected as the President of Delaware, an office he served until November 1781. During this time there was real contention over the ratification of the Articles of Confederation which consumed his energy. He was again elected to the Continental Congress in 1782 and 1783 but was unable to serve because of his poor health. In the fall of 1783 despite his poor condition, he was elected the Speaker of the Delaware General Assembly. He served as best he could but by the early spring of 1784, he became too weak to travel. The upper assembly voted to hold future meetings at Rodney's home, which they did for the next few weeks.

Caesar Rodney died at age fifty-six at his home near Dover on June 26, 1784, and was buried at "Poplar Grove," his home on the "Byfield" plantation. Rodney's will provided for the emancipation of his slaves. His grave, for some reason, went unmarked for over a hundred years. There are different opinions about where Rodney is buried. Some believe that in 1888, Rodney's remains were moved to Christ Episcopal Churchyard and an impressive twelve-foot granite monument was erected at this site by the National Sons of The American Revolution. Some believe that the remains moved weren't those of Caesar but of a relative. In Washington, D.C., near the Washington Monument, there is a memorial park and lagoon honoring the signers of the Declaration of Independence, and a granite block there bears the name of Caesar Rodney. There is also a statue of Rodney in Statuary Hall in the U.S. Capitol and a large equestrian statue, memorializing his famous ride, looms over Rodney Square in downtown Wilmington, Delaware.

Benjamin Rush
(1745–1813)

The Doctor in the House

Buried at Christ Church Burial Ground,
Philadelphia, Pennsylvania.

Declaration of Independence

By the age of thirty this Founder was already a prominent Philadelphia physician. In time he would be recognized as the most outstanding physician of his day. He is regarded as the father of American psychiatry. He founded Dickinson College and is one of the founders of Franklin and Marshall College. He also found the time to work as a leader for social and political reforms. He served in the Continental Congress and signed the Declaration of Independence. He was the surgeon general of the middle department of the Continental Army. During the ratification fight over the United States Constitution he championed the Federalist cause in Pennsylvania. In 1799 President John Adams appointed him to the position of Treasurer of the United States Mint. This accomplished Founder's name was Benjamin Rush.

Rush was born on Christmas Eve in 1745 near the city of Philadelphia. His father was a farmer and a gunsmith who passed away when his son was five years of age. His mother sent the boy to Maryland where he was raised by his uncle, Samuel Finley, who ran the West Nottingham Academy, a private school. It was his uncle who encouraged Rush to become a doctor. Rush first attended medical school at the College of Philadelphia and then travelled to England where he obtained his medical degree from the University of Edinburgh in 1768. A year later Rush returned to America and opened a medical practice in Philadelphia. He also

Portrait of Benjamin Rush by Thomas Sully, 1812.

taught chemistry at the College of Philadelphia where he wrote the first American text on chemistry.

In addition to practicing medicine, Rush wholeheartedly threw himself into the political turmoil brewing between England and the American colonies. He joined the Sons of Liberty and began writing essays advocating American independence. His political activities led to his appointment to the Second Continental Congress in 1776. He took his seat on July 20th which meant he had missed the chance to vote in favor of the Declaration of Independence but on August 2, 1776 he became one of the youngest signers of that document. Years later he described that moment in a letter to his good friend John Adams. Rush wrote, "Do you recollect the pensive and awful silence which pervaded the house when we were called up one after another, to the table of the President of Congress to subscribe what was believed by many at that time to be our own death warrants?"

The year 1776 was indeed a momentous one for Rush. In addition to signing the Declaration he was wed that January. The bride was the 17-year-old Julia Stockton who happened to be the daughter of Richard Stockton of Princeton, New Jersey. Thus Julia Stockton became unique as both the daughter and wife of a signer of the Declaration of Independence.

Rush was friends with the writer Thomas Paine and he encouraged Paine to publish the work *Common Sense.* Rush suggested the title for the politically influential piece which was a major factor in mobilizing colonial resistance to British rule. Rush was said to be relieved that there was someone beside himself who was willing to compose such an anti-British tract. Rush shared the sentiments expressed in Paine's work but feared that had he been the one to express them it would damage his image in Philadelphia.

In April of 1777 Rush was commissioned Surgeon General of the Middle Department of the Continental Army. Almost immediately Rush found himself in conflict with Dr. William Shippen, Jr., the director general of hospitals for the army. He blamed Shippen for the poor health conditions he witnessed in his new position. It is not an overstatement to say he was horrified by the health conditions that plagued the Continental Army. He then put these criticisms in writing. General Washington referred the matter to Congress which investigated and then dismissed the charges.

Rush had also written several letters critical of General Washington. In 1778 he sent a letter anonymously to the governor of Virginia, Patrick Henry. In the missive Rush expressed the view that the army would be better served if Washington was removed from command and replaced with Horatio Gates, Charles Lee, or Thomas Conway. The letter made its way to Washington who recognized the handwriting. Rush himself recognized that, as a result, the handwriting was on the wall and he resigned from the army and resumed his medical practice.

After the 1787 convention produced the Constitution, Rush became a strong proponent in favor of its ratification. He addressed Pennsylvania's ratifying convention saying that, "the hand of God was employed in this work, as that God had divided the Red Sea to give passage to the children of Israel." When the Constitution was ratified by the necessary number of states he proclaimed that it was, "as much the work of divine providence as any of the miracles recorded in the Old and New Testament were the effects of a divine power." Rush viewed the ratification as a sign that the heavens favored the Federalist side of the question.

In 1793 a yellow fever epidemic hit Philadelphia that killed at least 5,000 people. Rush worked tirelessly during this period often treating 100 patients in a single day. His methods which included bloodletting and purging were controversial but the work he performed made him a local hero. He had his critics who claimed his methods killed as many people as they saved. That said few could question his humanitarian efforts. He treated many patients for no charge and he established the first free medical clinic in America.

In 1799 President John Adams appointed Rush to the position of Treasurer of the United States Mint. It was a job he held until his death in 1813. He was laid to rest in the Christ Church Burial Ground in Philadelphia.

Rush left behind a legacy of social and political reforms. He had served as the President of the Pennsylvania Society for Promoting the Abolition of Slavery. He sided with and led reform movements aimed at eliminating public punishment and capital punishment. He advocated for a property tax to support public education. His was a life lived well in service to both the public and his nation.

Grave of Benjamin Rush at Christ Church Burial Ground in Philadelphia, Pennsylvania (photo by Joe Farley).

Roger Sherman

(1721 – 1793)

Three-Fifths Compromise

Buried at Grove Street Cemetery,
New Haven, Connecticut.

Continental Association • Declaration of Independence
Articles of Confederation • U.S. Constitution

Roger Sherman, of Connecticut, was the only person to sign all four founding documents of the United States of America: Continental Association, Declaration of Independence, Articles of Confederation, and Constitution. A lawyer and statesman, he with James Wilson proposed the Three-Fifths Compromise during the Constitutional Convention. Sherman later served as a member of the U.S. House of Representatives and as a U.S. Senator.

Sherman was born in Newton, Massachusetts, on April 19, 1721, to William Sherman and his second wife Mehetabel (née Wellington) Sherman. Others in his family tree include Senator, Secretary of the Treasury, and Secretary of State John Sherman (1823-1900), Civil War General William Tecumseh Sherman (1820-1891), and Senator William Maxwell Evarts (1818-1901), who was also Attorney General and Secretary of State.

William Sherman was variously a cordwainer, farmer, and shoemaker in Stoughton, Massachusetts. He married first Rebecca Cutler of Watertown with whom he had a son, William, who died in infancy. He then married Mehetabel Wellington of Watertown on September 3, 1715. Roger was born in 1721 and lived on the farm in Stoughton until 1743, studying his father's trades and never receiving a formal education. From pastor Reverend Samuel Dunbar, Roger privately learned the classics and theology. When William Sherman died in 1741, 18-year-old Roger cared for his widowed mother and the rest of the family.

Portrait of Roger Sherman by Ralph Earl, circa 1776.

In 1743, Roger literally followed in his older brother William's footsteps, setting out on foot with his cobbler's tools to find work in New Milford, Connecticut. Soon, a local attorney took notice of his writing ability and urged him to become a lawyer. In 1745, Sherman was named the surveyor of New Haven County, remaining in that position until 1752, after which he was the surveyor for Litchfield County until 1758. During this time, he turned his earnings and observations into great wealth through well-played land speculation.

Sherman married Elizabeth Hartwell of Stoughton, Massachusetts, in November 1749. The two had seven children, four of whom lived to adulthood. After Elizabeth passed in 1760 at the age of 34, Sherman moved to New Haven and married Rebecca Prescott in May 1763. The couple had eight children, seven of whom lived to adulthood.

Beginning in 1750, like Benjamin Franklin, Sherman began publishing a series of almanacs on a variety of subjects expressing his ideas and showcasing his writing ability. He studied law and was admitted to the Connecticut colonial bar in 1754. In 1755, he was elected to the Connecticut colonial Assembly, serving until 1766. He was also a justice of the peace for Litchfield County from 1755 to 1761. Later, he served in the state Senate (1766-1785), and as a judge of the Superior Court (1766-67 and 1773-88).

Beginning in the mid-1760s, Sherman was a leader in opposition to the British Parliament, personally urging protest of The Stamp Act. Though he was not initially one of the radical Sons of Liberty, he did eventually join the Committee of Correspondence to communicate with the other colonies following the Boston Tea Party.

As royal rule collapsed in Connecticut, Jonathan Trumbull was named the governor. He was a friend of Sherman's and named him one of 12 assistants including Eliphalet Dyer and William Samuel Johnson. For the first Continental Congress in 1774, Connecticut sent Sherman, Dyer, and Silas Deane.

In Philadelphia, Silas Deane was not impressed with his fellow delegate, writing in a letter to his wife, "Mr. Sherman is clever in private, but I will only say he is as badly calculated to appear in such Company as a chestnut-burr is for an eye-stone. He occasioned some shrewd countenances among the company, and not a few oaths, by the odd questions he asked, and the very odd and countrified cadence with which he speaks; but he was, and did, as well as I expected."

Sherman served in the Continental Congress from 1774 to 1781 and then again in 1784 during which he did more than Jefferson, or Adams, or any other delegate, signing the Continental Association, the Olive Branch Petition, the Declaration of Independence, the Articles of Confederation, and, eventually, as a delegate to the Constitutional Convention, the U.S. Constitution. He also wrote hundreds of letters, documents, and other correspondence "to establish regulations and restrictions on the trade of the United States; to regulate the currency of the country; to furnish supplies for the army; to provide for the expenses of the government; to prepare articles of confederation between the several states; and to propose a plan of military operations for the campaign of 1776."

Roger Sherman's biggest contribution in the Continental Congress may have been on June 11, 1776, when he was named to the committee to draft a declaration of independence from

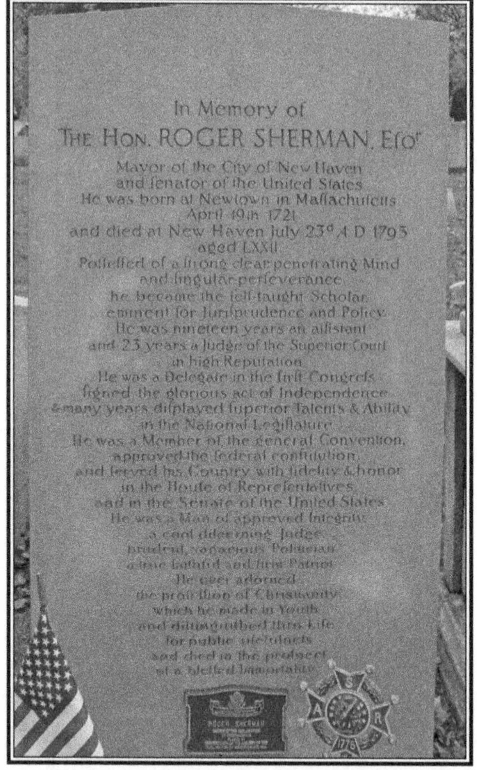

Grave of Roger Sherman at Grove Street Cemetery in New Haven, Connecticut (photo by Lawrence Knorr).

England along with Thomas Jefferson, John Adams, Benjamin Franklin, and Robert Livingston.

After the Revolution, Sherman was selected to represent Connecticut at the Constitutional Convention. He again played a prominent role as a key player in many votes. After the ratification of the Constitution, Sherman was elected to the First Congress (1789-1791). However, he did not quite finish his term, instead taking the vacant Senate seat of William Samuel Johnson on March 4, 1791.

In 1987, a draft of the Bill of Rights was found among James Madison's papers at the Library of Congress written in Sherman's hand. Historians have argued since over whether Sherman was a collaborator with Madison, or just made a copy for the record. According to Christopher Collier, the former Connecticut State

Historian, Sherman was simply making a copy. He had been against a Bill of Rights even after the draft was recorded.

Sherman served as a senator until his death at home in New Haven on July 23, 1793. He was 72. Sherman was buried at the New Haven Green. A few years after his death, a new cemetery was started a few blocks away to deal with the overcrowding under the Green. By 1821, many of the families had moved their loved ones' graves and headstones to the new cemetery. However, for thousands, this was not done. Only the headstones were moved, but the remains were not. Thus, perhaps 5,000 to 10,000 people remain buried under the New Haven Green. We believe some or all of Roger Sherman was moved to Grove Street Cemetery.

Richard Smith
(1735 – 1803)
Congressional Diarist

Buried at Unknown,
Natchez, Mississippi.

Continental Association

Richard Smith was a signer of the Continental Association during his service in the Continental Congress from 1774-1776 as a delegate from New Jersey. An attorney by trade, he is best known for his detailed diary kept regarding the proceedings. Smith was also briefly the Treasurer of New Jersey in 1776.

Born on March 22, 1735, Richard was the son of Richard "The Elder" and Abigail (nee Raper) Smith who resided in Burlington, New Jersey. The family were Quakers, descended from William Smith of Bramham Parish, West Riding, Yorkshire County in the 1500s. Richard "The Elder" was the first child of Samuel and Elizabeth Smith. He was born in Burlington, New Jersey on July 5, 1699, and died at Perth Amboy on November 9, 1751. He was a successful merchant who built and owned vessels involved in the sugar trade with the West Indies. The Smith sons would often accompany him on voyages.

Young Richard attended schools run by the Society of Friends, also known as the Quakers, as well as private tutors provided by his wealthy parents. He studied law under Joseph Galloway and was accepted into the Pennsylvania colonial bar in Philadelphia. He practiced law there for a while before returning to Burlington. In 1762 he married Elizabeth Rodman, with whom he had five children. On December 7, 1762, he was named the county clerk of Burlington County.

Portrait of Richard Smith etched from a silhouette, artist unknown.

In 1768, following the Treaty of Fort Stanwix with the Iroquois Confederacy, 69,000 acres between the Susquehanna and Mohawk rivers were ceded to New York. This is in what is now Otsego County. Smith and other speculators received large portions of this land. He decided to visit the tract with Robert Wells and others, keeping a detailed journal of the trip, including observations about the geography, economics, flora, fauna, and people of the area comprising the valleys of the Hudson, Mohawk, Susquehanna, and Delaware rivers. This journal was later published in 1906 as "A Tour of Four Great Rivers." Smith returned to the area many times and, in 1773, he built a house called "Smith Hall" on 4,000 acres on both sides of the Otsdawa Creek in what is now Laurens, New York.

While Richard followed a course of colonial and state offices, his brother Samuel followed in the father's footsteps as a successful merchant. Samuel did become the treasurer of the Western

Division of New Jersey and, in 1763, became a justice of the peace and then a member of the New Jersey Council. Later, he became the Treasurer of New Jersey. Samuel died suddenly in Burlington on July 13, 1776, while serving in this capacity at the age of 55. Richard returned to New Jersey to replace him in that role.

The New Jersey Committee of Safety elected Richard Smith as a delegate to the First Continental Congress on July 23, 1774. He was reelected on January 24, 1775, and February 14, 1776. He attended sessions from September 5, 1774 to October 26, 1774, May 10, 1775 to August 2, 1775 (except for his attendance of the New Jersey Assembly as clerk from May 15 to 20, 1775), September 12 to 30, 1775, and December 13, 1775, to March 30, 1776.

Smith kept a detailed diary of the events during these critical times, recording the events of September 1775 to March 1776. Along with the diaries of John Adams and Samuel Ward, it is one of the few personal records of these proceedings and provides insights not officially recorded.

As an example, on 12 September 1775, Smith wrote:

> I attended at Congress for the first Time since the Adjornment [sic]. Mr. [John] Hancock having a Touch of the Gout there was no President in the Chair. The Colonies of New Hampshire and N Carolina absent as also sundry Members from other Colonies. Dr. [Benjamin] Franklin read several Letters recieved [sic] today by Capt. Falkner from London and informed the Members that he had some Bales of Household Goods on Board of Falkner, desiring the Congress's Leave to land them. [N]o Objection to it only [Thomas] Willing [of Pennsylvania] and John Rutledge thought it irregular to do Business without a President and it was referred. Mr. Gadsden and others moved for an Adjornment [sic] to 10 Tomorrow, which was complyed [sic] with. 3 of the Georgia Delegates were present with Mr. Peyton Randolph and the new Delegates from Virginia, their Credentials not yet delivered, and little Business hitherto done this session.

It appears Smith spent a great deal of time listening and writing rather than speaking. There are few mentions of him in the proceedings except to say he was one of the delegates from New Jersey. Smith was from a conservative, mostly Loyalist section of his state. He signed the Continental Association on December 1,

This church is near the original city cemetery in Natchez, Mississippi where Richard Smith is likely buried in an unmarked grave (photo by Lawrence Knorr).

1774, putting in place economic sanctions against Great Britain. The following year, he did affix his name to the Olive Branch Petition on July 5, 1775, its aim to avoid war.

During his involvement with the New Jersey Provincial Congress in January 1776, he penned a letter to Lord Stirling, one of Washington's subordinates, regarding the treatment of prisoners of war, including 1000 dollars from the Continental Treasury to fund them.

A month before the Declaration of Independence, citing poor health (of his brother), Richard resigned his position with the Continental Congress and returned to New Jersey. John Hart took his place in the Congress and signed the Declaration. Following his brother's death, Smith focused on New Jersey, holding the position of Treasurer until he resigned on February 15, 1777. He returned to practicing law. In 1790, he moved his family to Laurens, Otsego County, New York, but returned to Philadelphia after less than ten years. His son, Richard R. Smith, was the first sheriff in the new Otsego County.

Around this time, he had developed a lingering illness. Upon the advice of his physician, Smith went on a trip to the South to improve his health. Unfortunately, while in Natchez, Mississippi on September 17, 1803, he passed away at the age of 68. For many years, there have been advertisements seeking information about the burial location of Richard Smith. While some believe he is interred in the Natchez City Cemetery, this institution did not exist until 1822. It is likely Smith was buried elsewhere and then possibly moved in 1822 with a number of other graves. If so, his grave remains unmarked.

"Smith Hall" was afterward known as "Otsego Hall" and was the early home of Fenimore Cooper, whose father had been an agent for the Smiths and had acquired the property from them.

Richard Stockton
(1730–1781)
A Most Ingenious Fellow

Buried at Stony Brook Quaker Meeting House Burial Grounds,
Princeton, New Jersey.

Declaration of Independence

This Founder was born into wealth and after graduating from the College of New Jersey in 1748 became a well known New Jersey lawyer. He was also treated well by the English crown who appointed him to the Royal Supreme Court of New Jersey. In his spare time, he collected works of art and bred horses. He recognized that as the troubles between England and the colonies grew he could lose everything, including his life if he opposed the crown. In 1776 he willingly joined other patriots in supporting American independence. New Jersey chose him to be one of their delegates to the Second Continental Congress. It was in this capacity that he affixed his signature to the Declaration of Independence. This action cost him his wealth and his health. It is no exaggeration to say that no signer suffered more for his autograph than Richard Stockton.

Stockton was born on October 1, 1730, near Princeton, New Jersey. His father, John Stockton, was a wealthy landowner who donated property to what is now Princeton University. After graduating college, Stockton studied law under David Ogden in Newark. In 1754 he was admitted to the bar and in 1763 he was made a sergeant of the law which was the highest degree in the field of law attainable at the time. During this period, he married the poet Annis Boudinot Stockton and the couple produced six children.

Portrait of Richard Stockton by John Wollaston.

Stockton was not your run of the mill revolutionary. His wife was an accomplished poet and the couple resided in his father's mansion located in Princeton. He loved both art and horses and spent much of his free time collecting the former and raising the latter. However, it appears that Stockton was impressed by the arguments made by those who favored a break with Britain. In time his views changed from Americans ruling themselves but pledging allegiance to King George to a total separation from the mother country. On July 2, 1776, as a member of the Continental Congress, Stockton voted yea on the question of independence. He was the first representative from New Jersey to sign the document Jefferson authored.

In the fall of 1776 Stockton and fellow signer George Clymer were sent to upstate New York to inspect the troops. The two were appalled at the lack of supplies, in particular the lack of adequate clothing for the troops. After hearing that the British army was approaching Princeton, Stockton returned to his home where, rather than gather his family and taking flight, he stayed and helped feed and clothe the American soldiers in the area. When those soldiers retreated, Stockton gathered his family and traveled to a home of a friend about thirty miles away in Monmouth County. A loyalist recognized Stockton and alerted others loyal to the British of his presence. He was roused from his sleep, taken prisoner, turned over to the English army, and eventually sent to Provost Prison in New York where he was starved and subjected to brutally freezing temperatures. Meanwhile, his estate in Princeton was occupied by General Cornwallis. All his household belongings and livestock were seized and his library burned. Anything that the British couldn't carry with them they destroyed.

When word reached Congress that Stockton was in prison and in failing health, a resolution was passed instructing General Washington to attempt to gain his release. While Washington did attempt to negotiate a prisoner exchange, it appears that Stockton was released only after signing a loyalty pledge in which he agreed to cease any war efforts against England.

Marker for Richard Stockton at Stony Brook Quaker Meeting House Burial Ground in Princeton, New Jersey (photo by Lawrence Knorr).

Stockton's time in prison did not kill him but it robbed him of his health. In a letter written in March of 1777, fellow Declaration signer John Witherspoon reported that Stockton was back home but was sick from "cold and exhaustion." Within a few years, he was stricken with cancer and underwent a painful operation to have a growth removed from his lip. The cancer eventually spread to his throat and he passed away at the age of 50 on February 28, 1781. He was laid to rest in the Stony Brook Quaker Meeting House Cemetery Grounds in Princeton New Jersey.

There are those who view Stockton as the only signer to recant the Declaration in order to gain his freedom. It is important to remember that after his release he again declared his loyalty to the United States. George Washington never harbored any ill feelings towards Stockton whom he considered a friend. After the signer from New Jersey passed away, Washington wrote his widow saying that she could rest assured that "we can never forget our friend . . ." Washington wished all Americans should never forget the sacrifices made and the hardships suffered by Richard Stockton in his service to his country.

Thomas Stone

(1743–1787)

Pacificist Patriot

Buried at Thomas Stone National Historic Site,
Port Tobacco, Maryland.

Declaration of Independence

Thomas Stone was a plantation owner and lawyer who represented Maryland in the Continental Congress and signed the Declaration of Independence. Later, he worked on the committee that created the Articles of Confederation and briefly acted as President of Congress in 1784.

Stone was born at "Poynton Manor" in Charles County, Maryland, the second son of David Stone and Elizabeth Jenifer Stone. He was the great great grandson of William Stone, the immigrant, who settled in Accomack County, Virginia, in 1628 and became a wealthy landowner and political leader including Governor of Maryland in 1648. In 1654 William moved the family to Maryland where he was given "Poynton Manor" for his services to Lord Baltimore. Thomas Stone's brothers, Michael J. Stone and John Hoskins Stone, also had important political careers. They were all the nephews of Daniel of St. Thomas Jenifer, through their mother.

Thomas grew up near the village of Welcome, Maryland, and was an ardent student. As a teenager, he rode ten miles on horseback to be tutored in Latin and Greek by a Scottish schoolmaster named Blaizedel. He subsequently studied law with Thomas Johnson in Annapolis, Maryland, and was admitted to the bar in 1764, at the age of 21. He then started a law practice in Frederick, Maryland, and represented clients circuit riding from Frederick to

Portrait of Thomas Stone by Robert Edge Pine, 1785.

Annapolis to Philadelphia. After a couple of years, he moved his law office back to Charles County.

At the age of 25, in 1768, Thomas married eighteen-year-old Margaret Brown, the daughter of Dr. Gustavus R. Brown and his second wife, Margaret Black Boyd. Stone received a dowry of one thousand pounds sterling with which he purchased a farm near the village of Port Tobacco, Maryland, which he named "Habre de Venture." Dr. Brown had a role in the founding of Charlestown at the head of the Port Tobacco Creek and built a home called "Rose Hill" which is on the National Register of Historic Places. His son, by the same name, followed in his father's footsteps and became a wealthy physician and close friend of George Washington. It was Dr. Gustavus Brown, Jr., the brother-in-law of Thomas Stone, who attended to the former President during his final illness at "Mount Vernon."

The young Stone family added three children: Margaret (1771-1809), Mildred (1773-1837), and Frederick (1774-1793). Upon the death of his father in 1773, the entire estate went to Thomas's older brother. This left Thomas with the increased responsibility of four younger brothers and two younger sisters in addition to his own three children. "Habre de Venture" was increased to accommodate the suddenly larger family.

To keep up with the expenses of his household, Stone continued his law practice and utilized his younger brother Michael to manage the plantation. At one point, Stone was involved in a lawsuit regarding a poll tax and the clergy and found himself on opposite sides from Samuel Chase and William Paca with whom he would later serve in the Continental Congress.

In 1774, Thomas joined the Charles County Committee of Correspondence, opposing British policies towards the colonies. From 1774 to 1776, he was a member of Maryland's Annapolis Convention, the body governing Maryland in the early days of the Revolution. In 1775, this convention sent Stone as a delegate to the Continental Congress where he and most of his fellow Marylanders initially favored reconciliation with Great Britain. He was a signer of the Olive Branch Petition that attempted to avoid hostilities. His views about the increasing tensions are expressed in this letter:

> I wish to conduct affairs so that a just and honorable reconciliation should take place, or that we should be pretty unanimous in a resolution to fight it out for independence. The proper way to effect this is not to move too quick. But then we must take care to do everything which is necessary for our security and defense, not suffer ourselves to be lulled or wheedled by any deceptions, declarations or givings out. You know my heart wishes for peace upon terms of security and justice to America. But war, anything, is preferable to a surrender of our rights.

Entering 1776, sentiment across the colonies moved towards independence. Stone wrote to his friend James Holyday,

> The die is cast. The fatal stab is given to any future connection between this country & Britain, except in the relation of conqueror & vanquished, which I can't think of without horror & indignation . . .

Stone was also moved towards independence despite the caution of many of his constituents. Representing Maryland, on May 15, 1776, he voted in favor of drafting a declaration of independence. This was soon followed by Richard Henry Lee's resolution for independence on June 7.

As the calendar turned to July, there was to be no peace settlement with England. The Maryland Convention had a change of heart and gave permission to the delegates to support independence. The vote was held July 4, 1776, with the Maryland delegation in the affirmative. Wrote Stone to the Maryland Council of Safety on July 12,

> May God send victory to the arm lifted in support of righteousness, virtue & freedom, and crush even to destruction the power which wantonly would trample on the rights of mankind.

Stone signed the Declaration of Independence on August 2, 1776.

Stone was elected a Maryland state senator in September and served in that capacity for several years. He also was assigned to the committee that drafted the Articles of Confederation but had to leave Philadelphia due to his wife taking ill after being vaccinated for smallpox, possibly due to the presence of mercury in the vaccine. Unfortunately, her health declined for the rest of her life, pulling Stone into seclusion as he cared for her.

Though elected to Congress in 1783, he retired after one term. He did remain active locally, practicing law in Annapolis, including participation in the Mount Vernon Convention in 1785. He was elected to the Constitutional Convention in 1787 but declined due to the deterioration of his wife's health. Margaret Stone finally succumbed to her long illness in 1787 at the age of thirty-six. Devastated, Thomas withdrew from public life.

Following her death, Stone was encouraged by his physicians to take a sea voyage. He began his preparations and headed to Annapolis. Before the vessel was to set sail, and only four months after Margaret's passing, on October 5, 1787, Thomas died of a "broken heart." He was only forty-four. He was buried in the family plot on his estate which is now managed by the National Park Service.

Said a fellow member in the Maryland state senate of Thomas Stone,

> . . . A talented writer. He was most truly a perfect man of business; he would often take the pen and commit to paper all the necessary writings of the Senate, and this he would do cheerfully while the other members were amusing themselves with desultory conversation; he appeared to be naturally of an irritable temper, still he was mild and courteous in his general deportment, fond of society and conversation, and universally a favorite from his great good humor and intelligence; he thought and wrote much as a professional man, and as a statesman, on the business before him in those characters; he had no leisure for other subjects; not that he was unequal to the task, for there were few men who could commit their thought to paper with more facility or greater strength of argument. There was a severe trial of skill between the Senate and the House of Delegates, on the subject of confiscating British property. The Senate for several sessions unanimously rejected bills passed by the house of delegates for that purpose: many, very long and tart, were the messages from

Grave of Thomas Stone at Thomas Stone National Historic Site in Port Tobacco, Maryland.

> one to the other body, on this subject; the whole of which, were on the part of the Senate, the work of Mr. Stone, and his close friend and equal in all respects, the venerable Charles Carroll of Carrollton.

There is a Thomas Stone High School in Charles County, Maryland. Stone's signature is memorialized on a boulder at the Memorial to the 56 Signers of the Declaration of Independence in the Constitution Gardens on the National Mall in Washington, D.C. Also, in the rotunda of the National Archives, there is a large mural entitled "The Declaration" painted by Barry Faulkner depicting about half of the signers. Stone is shown standing in the very back.

George Taylor
(1716–1781)

Indentured Ironmaster

Buried at Easton Cemetery,
Easton, Pennsylvania.

Declaration of Independence

George Taylor was a signer of the Declaration of Independence as a representative of Pennsylvania. He was born in Ireland in 1716 and was one of three signers of the Declaration born in Ireland. As a young man, he wanted to come to America but was too poor to pay his passage so he became an indentured servant to Samuel Savage who ran an iron foundry outside Philadelphia. Taylor went from being an indentured servant to a successful and respected businessman and citizen and signer of the historic Declaration of Independence.

He arrived in 1736 and started as a laborer, but when Savage discovered that Taylor had a certain degree of education, he made him a clerk in his foundry. In 1742, Savage died and George married his widow, Ann, and took over the iron business. It prospered. He and Ann would have two children. He also had five children with his housekeeper Naomi Smith with whom he would carry on an affair for years.

Taylor moved to Easton in 1763 and became involved in public affairs. In 1767, the same year Ann died, he purchased land and built an impressive home in Catasauqua, about fifteen miles from Easton. This home, the George Taylor Mansion, still stands and is a National Historic Landmark. He served in the provincial assembly from 1764 to 1769 and then was re-elected in 1775. There he helped draft the instructions to the delegates to the Continental Congress which called for voting against separation

Etching of George Taylor from the Pennsylvania Archives.

from Britain. As public sentiment changed, those instructions were rescinded in June 1776. As problems with Britain worsened Taylor spoke out in favor of independence. In July 1775, as colonial forces prepared for war, he was commissioned as a colonel in the Third Battalion of the Pennsylvania militia. Also in 1775, he went to work at Durham Iron Works, which he leased and produced grapeshot, cannonballs, bar shot, and cannons for the Continental Army. This diminished his wealth as he received limited compensation from a strapped government.

In 1776, the Continental Congress voted for independence on July 2 and adopted the Declaration of Independence on July 4. Before the vote for independence, five of Pennsylvania's delegates, all loyalists, were forced to resign as the Congress had passed a proposal that stated, "for our mutual security and protection" no man could remain in Congress without signing. On July 20, Taylor was among the replacements appointed by the assembly.

Others were Benjamin Rush, George Clymer, James Smith, and George Ross. One of his first duties was to affix his signature to the Declaration of Independence, which he did on August 2. The act of signing this momentous document was then considered an act of high treason against the British government and Crown. All the signers could be tried and executed and their property and estates confiscated

Of the 56 signers, he was one of only eight who were foreign-born, the only one to have been indentured, and the only iron-master. He was elected to the First Supreme Executive Council of Pennsylvania in 1777 but soon became ill and retired from public life.

After George Taylor resigned from public office, he continued to support the patriots. From 1777 to 1780, Taylor worked at his iron mills, making cannon-balls for the Continental Army. In 1780, Taylor became ill again and decided to return to his home in Easton. He spent the rest of his life there. He died on February 23, 1781, at the age of sixty-five. He sacrificed his estate for the Continental Army and did not live to see it's victory.

Grave of George Taylor at Easton Cemetery in Easton, Pennsylvania (photo by Joe Farley).

Taylor's body was originally buried at St. John's Lutheran Church in Easton. In 1854, a memorial was constructed in the Easton Cemetery for Taylor made of Italian marble. In 1870, his body was moved to the site of his memorial and was buried directly in front of it.

In Washington, D.C., near the Washington monument, is a small park and lagoon dedicated to the memory of the signers of the Declaration of Independence, and one of the granite blocks there bears the name of "George Taylor."

Nicholas Van Dyke
(1738–1789)
President of Delaware

Buried at Immanuel Episcopal Churchyard,
New Castle, Delaware.

Articles of Confederation

Colonial America politically and economically was dominated by the more populous areas that made up Massachusetts, Pennsylvania, and Virginia. During these times, the inhabitants of the smaller colonies looked to their leaders to protect their interests during the formation of the American nation. The small state of Delaware was represented by well-known patriots like Caesar Rodney, John Dickinson, and some lesser-known but just as able men. One of these lesser-knowns was Nicholas Van Dyke.

Van Dyke was born on September 25, 1738, in New Castle County near the present site of Delaware City. As a youth, he was educated at home before studying law in Philadelphia where he was admitted to the Pennsylvania Bar in1765. He then returned to New Castle where he began a law practice and married. His first wife died bearing the couple's first child in 1767. He remarried and had four additional children. One of his children would become a United States Senator and one grandchild a Congressman.

Showing an interest in the politics of the day, Van Dyke sided with the colonies in their conflicts with English rule. He was elected to Delaware's Boston Relief Committee in 1774 and, though viewed as a more conservative voice than that of Caesar Rodney, he still enjoyed the confidence of his fellow citizens as evidenced by his service at the Delaware Constitutional Convention of 1776. During the convention, Van Dyke worked closely with George Read, a signer of the Declaration of Independence, and those

Old postcard of Amstel House in New Castle, Delaware, the former home of Nicholas Van Dyke.

efforts gained him Read's lasting respect and admiration. He served in the state council at the same time and was appointed as Judge of Delaware's Admiralty Court.

In 1777 Van Dyke was elected to the Continental Congress replacing John Evans who declined to serve. While serving in Congress, he signed the Articles of Confederation. He did so despite his disagreement with the provision that permitted unlimited territorial expansion to the west for those states that had western frontiers. Van Dyke believed that these lands should be shared by all of the states in the Confederation.

In 1782 John Dickinson resigned as President (the equivalent of our current governors) of Delaware. The Delaware General Assembly voted to choose a successor. Van Dyke received 18 of the 30 votes cast and won the election. It's been said that one of his proudest moments while holding this office came on June 5, 1783, when he happily announced to the Assembly that the Treaty of Paris officially ending the Revolutionary War had been signed.

During his term as President of Delaware, Van Dyke's daughter married. Among the many friends who made the trip to attend the wedding was none other than George Washington. It is said that Washington enjoyed himself at the celebration so much that in addition to kissing the bride he made a point of kissing all the pretty women that had gathered at Van Dyke's home after the ceremony.

Van Dyke was President of Delaware at a time when he had to deal with Delaware's Revolutionary War debt. He devised a plan and successfully implemented the process by which his state paid off their portion of that debt. He also had to deal with the fate of a British loyalist named Cheney Chow. Chow had been tried on the charge of treason and acquitted but he was also charged with killing a member of the posse that had been sent to arrest him. Though the evidence against him was flimsy at best, Chow was convicted and sentenced to death in May of 1783. Van Dyke felt that pardoning Chow would destroy his political career but at the same time he was aware that many prominent citizens, including Caesar Rodney's brother Thomas, considered the condemned man innocent. Van Dyke handled the situation by postponing the execution indefinitely.

The worn tombstone of Nicholas Van Dyke at Immanuel Episcopal Churchyard, New Castle, Delaware.

After the end of his term as Delaware's President in 1786, Van Dyke resumed his law practice. He passed away on one of his farms on February 18, 1789, and was buried in a family plot on the property. His remains were later moved to the Immanuel Episcopal Church Cemetery in New Castle. Van Dyke's son Nicholas, Jr., represented Delaware in both the United States House of Representatives and the Senate. One of his grandsons Kensey Johns Jr. served in the U. S. House.

Joseph Warren
(1741–1775)
Hero of Bunker Hill

Buried at Forest Hills Cemetery,
Jamaica Plain, Massachusetts.

Military

Joseph Warren was a physician and Major General who was a key leader for liberty in Massachusetts at the outset of the American Revolution. He barely escaped death at Lexington and Concord and was subsequently martyred at the Battle of Bunker Hill where he fought as a private beside his men in the trench atop Breed's Hill rather than take overall command from the more experienced General Israel Putnam.

Joseph Warren was born June 11, 1741, in Roxbury, Massachusetts. He was the son of Joseph Warren, a farmer, and Mary (nee Stevens) Warren. The elder Warren fell from a ladder in their orchard and died when Joseph was only 14. Young Joseph attended the Roxbury Latin School and enrolled at Harvard College where he graduated in 1759 at the age of 18. He taught for a year and studied medicine. In September of 1764, he married an 18-year-old heiress Elizabeth Hooten. The two had four children: Elizabeth, Joseph, Mary, and Richard.

Joseph practiced medicine and surgery in Boston and was an avid Mason. Through his wife's connections, he had an interesting list of patients including John Adams and his family. Warren once saved 7-year-old John Quincy Adams' finger from amputation. He also had Loyalist patients such as the children of Thomas Hutchison and General Thomas Gage and his wife Margaret. It is the latter to whom some suggest he had an affair that gave him

Portrait of Joseph Warren by John Singleton Copley, 1765.

inside information about British military movements, but this is disputed.

Warren was also a leader of the patriot cause, writing an incendiary essay in the newspaper in 1768 under the pseudonym A True Patriot. His publishers were put on trial, but no jury would indict them.

Warren became Master of the Lodge in 1769 at the time Paul Revere was its Secretary. At this time, he also became involved in the Sons of Liberty, associating with John Hancock, Samuel Adams, and others. In February 1770, he performed an autopsy on the body of 12-year-old Christopher Seider who had been killed in Boston in a protest. The reaction to his funeral led to an uprising resulting in the Boston Massacre.

Following Elizabeth's death in 1772 at only 26, Joseph was a widower with young children. This did not dissuade him from his convictions. He authored a song "Free America" which was set to the melody of "The British Grenadiers." It was published in many colonial newspapers in 1774. As tensions rose around Boston, Warren was appointed to the Boston Committee of Correspondence. He spoke publicly at commemorations of the Boston Massacre, the last time in March 1775 while the city was occupied by the British. Warren drafted the Suffolk Resolves, endorsed by the Continental Congress, in resistance to the Coercive Acts. Following this, he was appointed President of the Massachusetts Provincial Congress—the highest position in the colony. Around this time he became engaged to Mercy Scollay.

On April 18, 1775, Warren got wind that the British were about to march on Concord, through Lexington, to capture the munitions stored there by the colonials. Warren sent William Dawes and Paul Revere on their rides that evening to warn Hancock and Adams in Lexington. The next morning, he left Boston and helped coordinate the militia alongside William Heath as the British returned to Boston. Warren was shot by a musket, the ball striking his wig without consequence.

When his mother learned of his brush with death, she begged him not to risk his life any further. Warren responded, "Where danger is, dear mother, there must your son be. Now is no time for any of America's children to shrink from any hazard. I will set her free or die." Warren continued to recruit and organize the militia while negotiating with General Gage as the leader of the Provincial Congress.

As the British continued to prepare to engage the colonials, Warren was commissioned as a major general by the Provincial Congress on June 14, 1775. A few days later, in the moments before the Battle of Bunker Hill, Warren arrived on the field as the militia was forming and asked where the heaviest fighting was likely to be. General Israel Putnam pointed to Breed's Hill. Warren then volunteered to join the fight as a private, leaving command with Putnam and Colonel William Prescott, who implored him not to do so. Both wished to serve him as their commander. Warren declined believing the two were more experienced as soldiers.

Warren joined the men in the trench atop Breed's Hill and helped hold the ranks against attacks from superior numbers. He declared to the British, "These fellows say we won't fight! By Heaven, I hope I shall die up to my knees in blood!" Warren continued to fight until out of ammunition. He remained to allow

Bronze statue of Joseph Warren at Forest Hills Cemetery in Jamaica Plain, Massachusetts (photo by Lawrence Knorr).

his militia to escape as the British made their third and final assault. Warren was killed instantly by a musket ball to the head, likely fired by Lieutenant Lord Rawdon who recognized him. His body was stripped and he was bayoneted repeatedly until unrecognizable. He was then shoved into a shallow ditch with another soldier. "I stuffed the scoundrel with another rebel into one hole, and there he is and his seditious principles may remain," said Captain Walter Laurie.

Said General Thomas Gage, the death of Warren was "worth the death of 500 men." In a letter to John Adams, Benjamin Hichborn described further damage inflicted on Warren's body two days after the battle by a Brit: "In a day or two after, Drew went upon the Hill again opened the dirt that was thrown over Doctor Warren, spit in his Face, jumped on his stomach, and at last cut off his head and committed every act of violence upon his body."

The next day his friend James Warren (no relation) wrote a letter to his wife, Mercy Otis Warren,

> . . . The British are reinforced but have not advanced, so things remain at present as they were we have killed many men & have killed & wounded about [six] hundred by the best accounts I can get. Among the first of which to our inexpressible grief is my friend Doctor Warren who was killed. it is supposed in the lines on the hill at Charlestown in a manner more glorious to himself than the fate of Wolf on the plains of Abraham. Many other officers are wounded and some killed. it is Impossible to describe the confusion in this place, women & children flying into the country, armed men going to the field, and wounded men returning from there fill the Streets.

Loyalist Peter Oliver wrote in 1782 that had Warren lived, George Washington would have been an obscurity. Military historian Ethan Rafuse wrote, "No man, with the possible exception of Samuel Adams, did so much to bring about the rise of a movement powerful enough to lead the people of Massachusetts to revolution."

Ten months after his death, his brothers and Paul Revere dug up and identified Warren's remains thanks to an artificial tooth

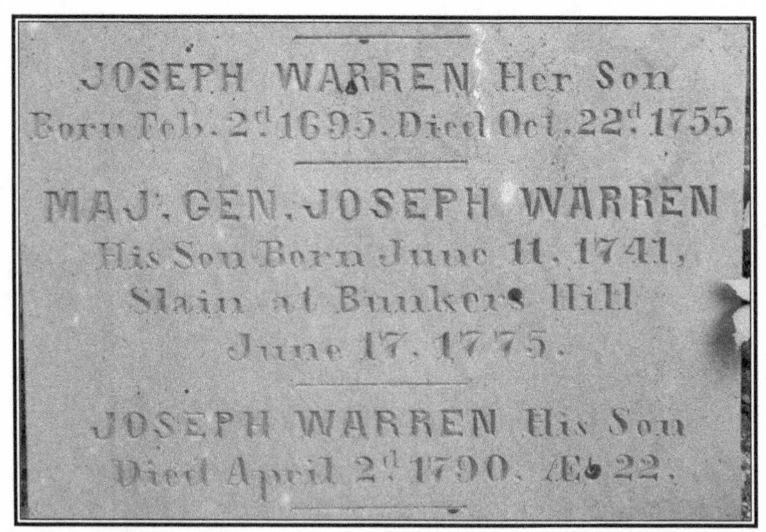

Marker for Joseph Warren at Forest Hills Cemetery in Jamaica Plain, Massachusetts (photo by Lawrence Knorr).

Revere had placed in the jaw. Warren was buried at the Granary Burying Ground in Boston. Later, in 1825, he was moved to St. Paul's Church before being placed in the family's vault at Forest Hills Cemetery in 1855, where he remains. Mercy Scollay continued to care for the Warren children and received assistance from John Hancock, Samuel Adams, Mercy Otis Warren, Benedict Arnold, and the Continental Congress. John Warren, Joseph's youngest brother, was a surgeon at Bunker Hill and for the rest of the war. He later founded Harvard Medical School and co-founded the Massachusetts Medical Society.

Warren is honored by at least four statues—three in Boston and one in Warren, Pennsylvania. Numerous towns, counties, and streets are named after him. Several ships have borne his name.

Anthony Wayne

(1716–1778)

Mad Anthony

Buried at Garrison Hill, Erie, Pennsylvania,
– and –
Old St. David's Church Cemetery,
Wayne, Pennsylvania.

Military

Anthony Wayne was one of the important military generals and statesmen who contributed extensively to the American Revolution. Had he not died suddenly at the age of 51, he might have given John Adams or Thomas Jefferson a real challenge for the presidency in 1796 and 1800.

Wayne was born on New Year's Day, 1745, in Chester County, Pennsylvania, and attended a private school in Philadelphia operated by his uncle. He eventually became an excellent surveyor and in 1765 was sent to Nova Scotia as a financial agent and surveyor in the service of a real estate company on the recommendation of Benjamin Franklin. He returned to the United States in 1767, married, and continued in his profession as well as serving in several local offices. In 1774, his father Isaac died and Anthony inherited his prosperous tannery business. Also that year, he was chosen as one of the provincial representatives to consider the relations between the colonies and Great Britain and was a member of the Pennsylvania convention that was held in Philadelphia to discuss this matter.

Wayne served in the Pennsylvania legislature in 1775. He was fond of military affairs. He began studying works on the art of war, and at the onset of the Revolutionary War raised a militia. In 1776, Wayne became colonel of the 4th Pennsylvania regiment.

Portrait of Anthony Wayne by Edward Savage.

He and his regiment were part of the Continental Army's failed invasion of Canada. He attacked the British at the Battle of Three Rivers and although wounded and defeated, withdrew his troops creditably and then was ordered to assume command at Fort Ticonderoga.

In February 1777, Wayne was commissioned a brigadier general. Prior to the war, Wayne had no military experience and other more experienced officers resented his quick advancement. He became known for his bravado and ill-advised attacks. He earned the nickname "Mad" Anthony Wayne because of his impulsive actions on the battlefield. Wayne was known for his fiery temper and would rather attack the enemy than avoid them.

Later in 1777, he assisted George Washington in the failed defense of the nation's capital, Philadelphia. He commanded troops at Brandywine, Germantown, and Paoli. The British surprise attack at Paoli on September 20, 1777, was a dark moment for Wayne. He lost a lot of men, and some of his officers thought he handled it poorly. Wayne's temper took hold, and he demanded first an official inquiry and then a full court-martial. The court-martial unanimously exonerated Wayne and acquitted him "with the highest honor." Washington heartily approved.

Washington relied heavily on Wayne throughout the war. Before making strategic decisions, it was Washington's habit to have his top general's write out their suggestions. He could always count on Wayne to propose aggressive and well-thought-out plans.

During the winter of 1777-78, Wayne did much to supply the American camp at Valley Forge. In March, he made a successful raid into British lines, capturing horses, cattle, and other needed supplies. In June of 1778, he led the American attack at the Battle of Monmouth. It was the first time Americans held their own in toe-to-toe battle with the British troops.

The highlight of Wayne's Revolutionary War service was his victory at Stony Point, New York on July 16, 1779. Washington had asked Wayne to form and command an elite "American Light Corps" (the equivalent of today's Special Forces). Wayne led his troops in a carefully planned, nighttime, surprise attack against a heavily fortified stronghold on top of a steep Hudson River palisade. The assault was successful and Wayne's troops captured the fort and its occupants. Wayne himself received a severe scalp wound. Before dawn, Wayne sent Washington a message that read: "The fort and garrison with Colonel Johnston are ours. Our officers and men behaved like men who are determined to be free."

The assault at Stony Point was widely recognized as one of the most brilliant maneuvers of the war. Congress unanimously passed resolutions praising Wayne and awarded him a gold medal commemorative. The Continental Army had experienced few successes. This victory, led personally by General Wayne, substantially improved the soldiers' morale.

In 1780, Wayne helped put down a mutiny of 1,300 Pennsylvania men who had not received payment from the government. He did so by serving as the men's advocate before the Confederation Congress, where he arranged an agreement to the advantage of the government and the satisfaction of the men.

In the summer of 1781, just before the Battle of Yorktown, Wayne saved a Continental Army force led by the Marquis de Lafayette from a trap set by the commander of the British Army, Lieutenant General Lord Cornwallis, near Williamsburg, Virginia.

The initial grave of Anthony Wayne in the blockhouse at Fort Presque Isle, Erie, Pennsylvania (picture by Joe Farley).

Wayne's small contingent of 800 Pennsylvanians was the vanguard of the continental forces. They were crossing over a swamp by a narrow causeway when they were ambushed by over 4,000 British. Instead of retreating, Wayne charged. The unexpected maneuver so surprised the enemy that they fell back confused allowing the rest of Lafayette's command to avoid the trap.

After the British surrender at Yorktown on October 19, 1781, Wayne went further south and severed the British alliance with Native American tribes in Georgia. He negotiated peace treaties with both the Creek and Cherokee, for which Georgia rewarded him with the gift of a large rice plantation. In October 1783 he was promoted to major general and retired from the Continental Army.

Wayne returned to Pennsylvania and resumed his civilian life. In 1784, he was elected to the general assembly from Chester County and served in the convention that ratified the Constitution of the United States. He then moved to Georgia and was elected to the Second United States Congress in 1791. He lost that seat during a debate over his residency qualifications and declined to run for reelection.

President Washington showed his high regard for Wayne once again in 1792 when he recalled him from civilian life and appointed Wayne as the commanding general of the newly-formed "Legion of the United States." At the end of the Revolutionary War, Great Britain agreed that the Mississippi River would be the western boundary of the United States and that the Great Lakes would be the northern border. Presumably, this meant British troops would withdraw from these areas into Canada. In fact, they did not. They encouraged and supplied a Western Indian Confederacy led by Blue Jacket of the Shawnees and Little Turtle of the Miamis. The Indians had achieved major victories over U.S. forces in 1790 under command of General Josiah Harmar and in 1791 under command of General Arthur St. Clair. More than 700 Americans died in the fighting.

Wayne recruited troops from the Pittsburgh area and established a basic training facility at Legionville to prepare the men of the "Legion of the United States" for battle. Located in Beaver County, Legionville was the first facility ever established to provide basic training for U.S. Army recruits.

In August 1794, Wayne mounted an assault on the Indian confederacy at the Battle of Fallen Timbers near Toledo, Ohio. It was a decisive victory for the U.S. forces and ended for all time the power of the British on American soil.

Wayne then negotiated the Treaty of Greenville between the Indian tribes and the United States. The treaty was signed in August 1795 and gave most of what is now Ohio to the United States. He returned home to a hero's welcome in the Philadelphia area.

In June 1796, Wayne was back in the frontier overseeing the surrender of British forts to the U.S. In a visit to Fort Presque Isle in Erie, Pennsylvania, he suffered a serious gout attack. There were no physicians at the fort and calls went out to Pittsburgh and the Army hospitals. Unfortunately, help arrived too late, and Anthony Wayne died on December 15, 1796.

A year earlier at Fort Presque Isle, to assist in defending against attacks from Native Americans, 200 Federal troops from Wayne's army under the direction of Captain John Grubb built a blockhouse on a bluff there known as Garrison Hill. Wayne had requested that upon his death he be buried there. When he died, his body was placed in a plain oak coffin, his initials and date of death were driven into the wood using round-headed brass tacks, and his request was honored. He was buried at the foot of the blockhouse's flagstaff on Garrison Hill.

Twelve years later, Wayne's son, Isaac, rode to Erie in a small, two-wheeled carriage called a sulky. He came (at the urging of his sister Peggy) to bring his father's remains back to be buried in the family plot at St. David's Church about 400 miles away outside of Philadelphia. Young Wayne enlisted the help of Dr. J. G. Wallace, who had been with Mad Anthony at the Battle of Fallen Timbers and at his side when he died.

When Wallace opened Wayne's coffin, he found little decay except in the lower portion of one leg. This caused a dilemma, as Isaac did not have enough space to transport the entire body. He expected to put bones in boxes on his sulky. Dr. Wallace used a custom common to American Indians to solve the dilemma. He dismembered the body and boiled it in a large iron kettle until the flesh dropped off. He cleaned the bones and packed them into Isaac's boxes. The task was so distasteful that Dr. Wallace threw the remaining tissue and his instruments into the coffin and closed the grave. Isaac Wayne made the long journey across Pennsylvania with his father's bones in the back of his sulky. The bones were interred at Old St. David's Church Cemetery with funeral rites celebrated on July 4, 1809. A huge crowd attended.

General Anthony Wayne is well-memorialized. He has a long list of cities, towns, and municipalities named after him, including 15 states that have a Wayne County. In Pennsylvania, there is a Wayne County as well as a Waynesboro and a Waynesburg. He has schools, bridges, a university (Wayne State University in Detroit), a brewing company (Mad Anthony Brewing Co. in Fort Wayne, Indiana), an ale (Mad Anthony Ale, a product of Erie Brewing Co.), a hotel (General Wayne Inn in Merion, PA), parks, hospitals, and even a barbershop named in his honor. There is a large statue in Fort Wayne, Indiana, as well as a gilded bronze equestrian statue at the Philadelphia Museum of Art and one at Valley Forge. In 1929, the U.S. Post Office issued a stamp honoring Wayne and commemorating the 150th anniversary of the Battle of Fallen Timbers.

Anthony Wayne's strange interment has given rise to a popular ghost story. It was a long, tough trip from Erie to Wayne over 380 miles of unpaved roads of what is now Route 322. The story goes that Isaac had many problems along the way and that the trunk kept falling off and breaking open, losing bones along the way. Some claim that on each New Year's Day (Wayne's birthday), his ghost rises from his grave in Wayne and rides across the state searching for his missing bones. The kettle used to boil Wayne's body and the dissection instruments used by Dr. Wallace are on display at the Erie County History Center on State Street in Erie.

The final resting place of the bones of Anthony Wayne at Old Saint David Church Cemetery in Wayne, Pennsylvania (photo by Joe Farley).

Noah Webster
(1758–1843)
Man of Many Words

Buried at Grove Street Cemetery,
New Haven, Connecticut.

Thought Leader

Although Noah Webster hasn't uttered a syllable since his death on May 28, 1843, to this day many people still introduce the definition of a word with the phrase "Webster says." As a matter of fact, Webster's fame and name have become so associated with "dictionary" that his other accomplishments have been overshadowed by the creation that still bears his name. In 2006, John Morse, president, and publisher of Merriam-Webster, Inc. noted that because of his work as a dictionary maker Webster "is probably one of the least known of the Founding Fathers." Morse also pointed out that Webster was one of the most influential thinkers in the period leading up to the 1787 Constitutional Convention saying, "Just about every delegate had read his 1785 tract *Sketches on American Policy* and was influenced by it." Among the recommendations in the work was the establishment of a constitutional government that included a Congress.

Noah Webster was born on October 16, 1758, in West Hartford, Connecticut. His father was a descendant of John Webster a former Connecticut Governor and his mother was a descendant of William Bradford who was Governor of the Plymouth Colony. Webster attended school in a one-room schoolhouse. He would later describe the teachers there as the "dregs of humanity" and this early experience with education would serve to inspire and motivate him to improve the educational opportunities for the generations that would follow him.

Portrait of Noah Webster by Samuel Finley Breese Morse.

Webster enrolled at Yale College shortly before he turned 16. His four years at Yale coincided with the American Revolution and the young student served in the Connecticut militia. After graduation, he studied law under a future United States Supreme Court Chief justice Oliver Ellsworth. During this period, he was also teaching school full time, a schedule he found impossible to manage, so he abandoned the study of law for a year and did not pass the bar examination until 1781.

It was around this time that Webster turned his attention to writing for a New England newspaper. His stories championed the Revolution and set forth the argument that the American separation from England was permanent. His work brought him to the attention of many prominent Americans including George Washington and Benjamin Franklin. These and other American leaders corresponded with Webster sharing ideas on the new nation. Years before these leaders met to form a new United States government Webster wrote: "So long as any individual state has power to defeat the measures of the other twelve, our pretended union is but a name, and our confederation, a cobweb."

When the Philadelphia Convention sent the Constitution to the states for ratification, Webster became an ardent supporter of the document. In 1787 he wrote a pamphlet titled *An Examination into the Leading Principles of the Federal Constitution Proposed by the Late Convention Held at Philadelphia.* His arguments favoring ratification proved influential throughout the states. He also expressed his feelings on the first ten amendments to the Constitution, the Bill of Rights, when he wrote: "paper declarations of rights are trifling things and no real security to liberty." His thoughts on the subject reflected the feelings of many other Founders including Richard Henry Lee and Elbridge Gerry.

Webster married Rebecca Greenleaf in 1789 and the couple would produce eight children. The family would eventually settle in New Haven, Connecticut where Webster would aid in the founding of Amherst College. Webster's marriage followed a series of failures in the romantic realm at least one of which led to a depressive state that he worked himself out of through his writing.

Alexander Hamilton lent Webster $1,500 in 1793 so he could move to New York City to edit the leading Federalist newspaper that supported the policies proposed by the Washington Administration. In this role, he was repeatedly criticized by the supporters of Thomas Jefferson who referred to him as "a deceitful newsmonger" and "an incurable lunatic." He also endured critics among fellow Federalists who accused him of harboring pro-French views. While it was true that Webster was influenced by the French theorist Jean-Jacques Rousseau, he also urged that the United States remain neutral when war broke out between England and France in 1793. He also opposed the French foreign minister Citizen Genet for setting up clubs or societies whose purpose was to attack President Washington's neutrality proclamation. Webster advised his fellow Federalist writers to ignore the clubs. He predicted that peace would render them obsolete.

With time, Webster's influence as a Founder was overshadowed by his contributions to American education. His three-volume work titled *A Grammatical Institute of the English Language* included the Webster speller which taught children in America to read, spell, and pronounce words for generations. Referred to by most as the "Blue-Backed Speller," by 1890 its sales totaled 60 million. His dictionary, first published in 1806 though not completed until 1825, contained seventy thousand words and twelve thousand of these had never before appeared in such a work. In May of 1843, he completed work on revising the appendix to the dictionary's second edition. A few days later, on the 23rd of the month at the age of 84, he passed away. He was laid to rest in the Grove Street Cemetery in New Haven.

Noah Webster is certainly not forgotten largely due to his work on the dictionary that still bears his name. The same cannot be said for his work as one of the nation's Founders given his influence on the thinking of men like Franklin, Washington, and James Madison. Indeed, one could argue that Madison would not have been off-base had he begun some of the arguments he made at the Constitutional Convention with the words "Webster says."

Grave of Noah Webster at Grove Street Cemetery in New Haven, Connecticut (photo by Lawrence Knorr).

Henry Wisner
(c 1720–1790)
Gunpowder Patriot

Buried at Old Wallkill Cemetery,
Phillipsburg, New York.

Continental Association • Finance

Henry Wisner was a patriot leader during the American Revolution and represented New York in the Continental Congress. If he hadn't hurried home to Goshen, New York right after the vote for independence, to make gunpowder for the coming hostilities, he likely would have signed the Declaration of Independence on August 2. His story is a bit unusual.

The precise date of his birth is unknown but was around 1720 in Florida, New York, a little village in Orange County. Wisner lived his entire life as a resident of Orange County. His family originally came to America from Switzerland in 1710. Henry married Sarah Norton from Queens County on Long Island, probably around 1740 and they settled in Goshen, New York where he built and operated a gristmill and became one of the town's leading citizens. Although he received the ordinary local education he was trusted and was appointed the justice of the peace.

In 1759, he was elected a member of the Colonial Assembly of New York and continued to serve there for eleven consecutive terms until 1769. He was a member of the first county committee to consider the difficulty between Great Britain and the American colonies. In 1768, he became a judge in the county's court of common pleas. His zeal led him to be named a delegate from Orange County, to the first Congress which convened at Philadelphia, in the fall of 1774. When New York created a revolutionary government in 1775, Wisner was sent to the New

Monument in honor of Henry Wisner in Goshen, New York (photo by Lawrence Knorr).

York Provincial Congress. That body named him a delegate to the Second Continental Congress, where he served until 1776.

New York, at this time, was clearly anxious to maintain peace and doubtful of the policy of independence. In December, the New York Convention had voted that only five of the twelve delegates that had originally been appointed, should continue at Philadelphia and that any three should be considered a quorum to represent the colony. On June 8, 1776, the delegates wrote home for instructions and were told they had no authority to vote for a break with England. On July 2, twelve of the thirteen colonies voted that the united colonies are free and independent states. Every other hesitating colony had withdrawn its instructions or left its delegates free to follow the general feeling, strongly in favor of independence. The New York delegation feeling the awkwardness of their position wrote to the Congress of New York

Grave of Henry Wisner at Old Wallkill Cemetery in Phillipsburg, New York (photo by Lawrence Knorr).

and explained that there was not a single dissenting vote for independence. The New York delegates had not voted on July 2 and were silent again on the formal adoption of the declaration on July 4. Finally, on July 9, New York's Congress reversed its instructions and on August 2, it was signed by all the delegates then present. Wisner had left Philadelphia and was not present on that occasion. A claim made years later and stated on the monument in Goshen that Wisner was the only member of the New York delegation to vote in favor of independence seems to be without foundation. He did not vote because he could not vote.

Wisner had learned while serving in Congress that the Continental Army was desperate for powder and shot. When he returned home he built three gunpowder mills. At their height, he was shipping 1,000 pounds of gunpowder to the Army each week. He later financed the erection of cannon and other defensive works overlooking the Hudson River that blocked the British ability to use the river. Both the Americans and the British knew that passage on the Hudson was strategically important. In late 1776, Wisner along with Gilbert Livingston sounded the Hudson River, and as part of a Secret Committee of the Committee of Safety, recommended the placement of chains in strategic locations along the Hudson. The Americans eventually constructed such chains. The largest and most important was the Great Chain between West Point and Constitution Island which was reset each spring until the end of the war.

In 1777, while serving in the provincial congress, Wisner served as a member of the committee that drafted the first constitution of the state of New York. Under that constitution, he served as a state senator from 1777 until 1782. In 1788, Wisner was a delegate to the state convention called to ratify the U.S. Constitution. He was one of those who opposed ratification fearing too much power was granted to the central government, which would eventually infringe on individual rights.

Henry Wisner died at home in Goshen in 1790 and is buried in the Old Wallkill Cemetery in Phillipsburg, New York. At this writing, his grave is very badly weather-beaten and his name can barely be made out on the stone. There is nothing around his grave that tells anything about him. As mentioned above there is a nice monument to his memory in Goshen on which is the claim that he was the only New Yorker who voted for the Declaration of Independence.

George Wythe
(1726–1806)
The Law Professor

Buried at St. John's Episcopal Churchyard,
Richmond, Virginia.

Declaration of Independence

George Wythe was at one time the most respected and revered man in Virginia if not in the whole United States. He was America's first law professor and a close friend and mentor of Thomas Jefferson, James Monroe, John Marshall, and Henry Clay. He was a signer of the Declaration of Independence and a delegate to the 1787 Philadelphia Convention. He left the convention before the signing of the U.S. Constitution to tend to his dying wife. He played an important role at the Virginia Ratifying Convention and over the years grew to hate slavery and freed his slaves. He was murdered by his great-nephew George Sweeney in 1806 although Sweeney was found "not guilty" when tried.

It all began in 1726 when George Wythe was born in what is now Hampton, Virginia. His father died when he was three. His mother Margaret Walker Wythe instilled in him a love of learning and homeschooled him until he was sixteen. At that age, he began to study law in the office of his uncle Stephen Dewey. George was admitted to the bar in 1746 the same year his mother died. Early in 1748, he married Ann Lewis, who died eight months later. The bereaved widower settled in Williamsburg to teach and practice law.

Wythe got his first taste of public service in 1748 when he was appointed a clerk for two important committees of the House of Burgess. In 1750 he was elected a Williamsburg alderman and in 1754 elected to the House of Burgess.

Etching of George Wythe by an unknown artist.

Shortly after in 1755, he married Elizabeth Taliaferro. Her father Richard built them a house in Williamsburg which is still called the George Wythe House and is open to the public.

In 1762 a college professor friend William Small introduced Wythe to Thomas Jefferson and suggested Wythe supervise Jefferson's legal training. He agreed and a lifelong friendship ensued. Wythe continued his thriving legal practice with Jefferson's assistance and in 1767, Wythe introduced Jefferson to the bar of the General Court, and he himself was appointed as clerk to the House of Burgess.

In 1764, Wythe wrote the original Virginia protest against the Stamp Act. It was so fiery that it had to be rewritten in a softer tone to gain approval. It didn't hurt his popularity however as he was elected Mayor of Williamsburg in 1768.

On May 10, 1775, the Second Continental Congress convened in Philadelphia. Wythe was elected as a delegate to replace George Washington, who took command of the continental army. He was very active at the Congress and voted for the Declaration of Independence. The historic document was not ready for signing until August 2 and by that time Wythe had returned to Williamsburg, thus he and other absent delegates signed later. He signed the document in September. His signature appears first among the Virginia signatures. He was so highly respected by his fellow Virginians that the other delegates left a space so that his signature would be first. The signers' names were not made public until the following January, for all knew the Declaration was an act of treason, punishable by death.

Wythe taught for over twenty years at the College of William and Mary. In 1779, Wythe was appointed to the nation's first law professorship, established at the college by his former student Thomas Jefferson.

In 1787 Wythe became one of Virginia's delegates to the Constitutional Convention. He, Alexander Hamilton, and Charles Pinckney served on the committee which established the Convention's rules and procedures. He left the Convention early before the signing took place to tend to his dying wife Elizabeth. She died later that year.

The following year, he was one of the Federalist leaders at the Virginia ratifying convention. There he presided over the Committee of the Whole and offered the resolution for ratification. He helped to sway the delegates to support the new constitution and Virginia narrowly became the tenth state to ratify it.

Over the years Wythe had grown to hate slavery, and after his second wife Elizabeth died, he began to free his slaves. He lived with two of his former slaves: a housekeeper Lydia Broadnax, and a young man named Michael Brown. Wythe was so fond of Michael that he named him to inherit a part of his estate. Also living with him was his great-nephew, George Wythe Sweeney. Sweeney, who was in line to inherit most of the estate was a ne'er-do-well who ran up huge gambling debts and had forged his uncle's name on checks and stolen from him to cover his debts. Hoping to avoid detection and inherit the entire estate, he resorted to murder. He poisoned coffee, most probably with arsenic, that George Wythe, Michael Brown, and Lydia Broadnax drank. George and Michael both died from the poison but Lydia survived. Sweeney was indicted for murder. There was plenty of evidence against Sweeney, but by Virginia law, blacks could not testify against whites in court, so Lydia was not heard, and Sweeney was found "not guilty" of murder. Wythe died a slow and painful death on June 8, 1806.

Wythe's funeral was the largest in state history until that time. Richmond businesses closed for the day, and thousands lined the funeral route. The service was conducted at the state capitol. He was buried at St. John's Episcopal Churchyard in Richmond, the church in which Patrick Henry made his famous "give me liberty or give me death" speech.

In his will, Wythe left his large book collection to Thomas Jefferson which he later sold to create the Library of Congress. There is a Wythe Avenue in Richmond and the law school at the College of William and Mary is named the Marshall-Wythe School of Law. His home in Williamsburg, as previously mentioned, operates as a museum.

Grave of George Wythe in Saint Johns Episcopal Churchyard in Richmond, Virginia (photo by Lawrence Knorr).

Sources

Books, Magazines, Journals, Files:

Appleby, Joyce. *Inheriting the Revolution: The First Generation of Americans.* Cambridge, Massachusetts: Harvard University Press, 2000.

Bordewich, Fergus M. *The First Congress: How James Madison, George Washington, and a Group of Extraordinary Men Invented the Government.* New York: Simon and Schuster Paperbacks, 2016.

Bowen, Catherine Drinker. *Miracle at Philadelphia: The Story of the Constitutional Convention May to September 1787.* Boston, Massachusetts: Little, Brown & Company, 1966.

Brookhiser, Richard. *Gentleman Revolutionary: Gouverneur Morris The Rake Who Wrote the Constitution.* New York: Free Press, 2003.

Chadwick, Bruce. *I Am Murdered: George Wythe, Thomas Jefferson, and the Killing That Shocked a New Nation.* Hoboken, New Jersey: John Wiley & Sons, 2009.

Chambers, II, John Whiteclay. *The Oxford Companion to American Military History.* Oxford: Oxford University Press, 1999.

Commager, Henry Steele & Richard B. Morris. *The Spirit of 'Seventy-Six: The Story of the American Revolution as Told by Participants.* New York: Harper & Rowe, 1967.

Conlin, Joseph R. *The Morrow Book of Quotations in American History.* New York: William Morrow and Company, Inc., 1984.

Daniels, Jonathan. *Ordeal of Ambition.* Garden City, New York: Doubleday & Company, Inc., 1970.

Dann, John C. *The Revolution Remembered: Eyewitness Accounts of the War for Independence.* Chicago: University of Chicago Press, 1980.

DeRose, Chris. *Founding Rivals: Madison vs. Monroe: The Bill of Rights and the Election that Saved a Nation.* New York: MJF Books, 2011.

Ellis, Joseph J. *Revolutionary Summer: The Birth of American Independence.* New York: Alfred A. Knopf, 2013.

———. *The Quartet: Orchestrating the Second American Revolution, 1783-1789.* New York: Alfred A. Knopf, 2015.

———. *His Excellency: George Washington.* New York: Alfred A. Knopf, 2004.

Fleming, Thomas. *Duel: Alexander Hamilton, Aaron Burr and the Future of America.* New York: Basic Books, 1999.

Flexner, James Thomas. *George Washington in the American Revolution, 1775-1783.* Boston: Little, Brown & Company, 1967.

Flower, Lenore Embick. "Visit of President George Washington to Carlisle, 1794." Carlisle, Pennsylvania: The Hamilton Library and Cumberland County Historical Society, 1932.

Griffith, IV, William R. *The Battle of Lake George: England's First Triumph in the French and Indian War.* Charleston, South Carolina: The History Press, 2016.

Grossman, Mark. *Encyclopedia of the Continental Congress*. Armenia, New York: Grey House Publishing, 2015.

Hamilton, Edward P. *Fort Ticonderoga: Key to a Continent*. Boston: Little, Brown & Company, 1964.

Isenberg, Nancy. *Fallen Founder: The Life of Aaron Burr*. New York: Penguin Group, 2007.

Kennedy, Roger G. *Burr, Hamilton, and Jefferson: A Study in Character*. New York: Oxford University Press, 1999.

Kiernan, Denise & Joseph D'Agnese. *Signing Their Lives Away: The Fame and Misfortune of the Men Who Signed the Declaration of Independence*. Philadelphia: Quirk Books, 2008.

———. *Signing Their Lives Away: The Fame and Misfortune of the Men Who Signed the United States Constitution*. Philadelphia: Quirk Books, 2011.

Klarman, Michael J. *The Framers' Coup: The Making of the United States Constitution*. New York: Oxford University Press, 2016.

Langguth, A. J. *Patriots*. New York: Simon and Schuster, 1988.

Larson, Edward J. *A Magnificient Catastrophe*. New York: Free Press, 2007.

Lee, Mike. *Written Out of History: The Forgotten Founders Who Fought Big Government*. New York: Penguin Books, 2017.

Lomask, Milton. *Aaron Burr: The Years from Princeton to Vice President, 1756-1805*. New York: Farrar Straus Giroux, 1979.

Maier, Pauline. *American Scripture: Making the Declaration of Independence*. New York: Alfred A. Knopf, Inc., 1997.

McCullough, David. *John Adams*. New York: Simon & Schuster, 2002.

Middlekauff, Robert. *The Glorious Cause: The American Revolution, 1763-1789*. Oxford: Oxford University Press, 2005.

Miller, Jr., Arthur P. & Marjorie L. Miller. *Pennsylvania Battlefields and Military Landmarks*. Mechanicsburg, Pennsylvania: Stackpole Books, 2000.

Millett, Allan R. & Peter Maslowski. *For the Common Defense: A Military History of the United States of America*. New York: The Free Press, 1984.

Moore, Charles. *The Family Life of George Washington*. New York: Houghton Mifflin, 1926.

Nagel, Paul C.. *The Lees of Virginia: Seven Generations of an American Family*. Oxford: Oxford University Press, 1990.

Racove, Jack N. *Revolutionaries: A New History of the Invention of America*. New York: Houghton Mifflin Harcourt, 2011.

Raphael, Ray. *Founding Myths: Stories That Hide Our Patriotic Past*. New York: MJF Books, 2004.

Rossiter, Clinton. *1787 The Grand Convention*. New York: The Macmillan Company, 1966.

Schweikart, Larry & Michael Allen. *A Patriot's History of the United States from Columbus's Great Discovery to the War on Terror*. New York: Penguin, 2004.

Sedgwick, John. *War of Two: Alexander Hamilton, Aaron Burr and the Duel That Stunned The Nation*. New York: Berkley Books, 2015.

Sharp, Arthur G. *Not Your Father's Founders*. Avon, Massachusetts: Adams Media, 2012.

Taafee, Stephen R. *The Philadelphia Campaign, 1777-1778.* Lawrence, Kansas: University of Kansas Press, 2003.
Ward, Matthew C. *Breaking the Backcountry: The Seven Years' War in Virginia and Pennsylvania, 1754-1765.* Pittsburgh, Pennsylvania: University of Pittsburgh Press, 2003.
Weisberger, Bernard A. *America Afire: Jefferson, Adams, and the Revolutionary Election of 1800.* New York: HarperCollins, 2000.
Williams, Roger M. "Who's Got Button's Bones?" *American Heritage.* Volume 17, Issue 2 (February 1966).
Wood, Gordon S. *The Radicalism of the American Revolution.* New York: Vintage Books, 1993.
———. *Empire of Liberty: A History of the Early Republic, 1789-1815.* New York: Penguin Books, 2004.
———. *Revolutionary Characters: What Made the Founders Different.* New York: Penguin Books, 2006.
———. *The Americanization of Benjamin Franklin.* Oxford: Oxford University Press, 2009.
Wright, Benjamin F. *The Federalist: The Famous Papers on the Principles of American Government: Alexander Hamilton, James Madison, John Jay.* New York: Metro Books, 2002.
Young, Alfred F. *Masquerade: The Life and Times of Deborah Sampson, Continental Soldier.* New York: Alfred A. Knopf, 2004.
———. *The Shoemaker and the Tea Party: Memory and the American Revolution.* Boston: Beacon Press, 1999.
Zobel, Hiller B. *The Boston Massacre.* New York: W. W. Norton & Company, 1970.

Video Resources:
Guelzo, Allen C. *The Great Courses: America's Founding Fathers (Course N. 8525).* Chantilly, Virginia: The Teaching Company, 2017.

Online Resources:
Archives.gov – for information on the Constitutional Convention.
CauseofLiberty.blogspot.com – for information on Daniel Carroll.
ColonialHall.com – for information about the signers of the Declaration of Independence.
DSDI1776.com – for information on many Founders.
FamousAmericans.net – for information on many Founders.
FindaGrave.com – for burial information, vital statistics and obituaries.
FirstLadies.org – for information on Abigail Adams.
Newspapers.com – Hundreds of newspaper articles were accessed—too numerous to mention here.
NPS.gov – for information on various park sites.
TeachingAmericanHistory.com – for information on Charles Pinckney and George Wythe.
TheHistoryJunkie.com – for information on multiple Founders.
USHistory.org – for information on multiple Founders.
Wikipedia.com – for general historical information.

Index

INDEX

INDEX

INDEX

INDEX

Coming soon ....

Graves of Our Founders:

Volume 2
Volume 3
Volume 4

Also available from these authors:

The Keystone Tombstones series about famous graves found in Pennslvania:

Volume 1
Volume 2
Volume 3
Sports
Best of Keystone Tombstones
Civil War
Philadelphia Region
Anthracite Region
Susquehanna Valley
Pittsburgh Region
Battle of Gettysburg

The Gotham Graves series about famous graves found in New York City:

Volume 1
Volume 2

The Murders, Massacres, and Mayhem in the Mid-Atlantic series:

Volume 1

BY JOE FARRELL:

Jesus Runs Away ... and other stories of attending Catholic schools in the early 60s

BY JOE FARLEY:

Trumpet Call to Victory: The Final Years of Hazelton Saint Gabriel's Basketball

Song Poems in Search of Music

BY LAWRENCE KNORR:

Gettysburg Eddie: The Story of Eddie Plank

Wonder Boy: The Story of Carl Scheib

CPSIA information can be obtained
at www.ICGtesting.com
Printed in the USA
LVHW042316040320
648984LV00004B/821

9 781620 061763